THE HISTORY OF
CORPORAL PUNISHMENT

GEORGE RYLEY SCOTT

SENATE

The History of Corporal Punishment

First published in 1968 as *Flagellation* by Tallis Press Ltd,
London.

This edition first published in 1996 by Senate, an imprint of
Random House UK Ltd, Random House, 20 Vauxhall Bridge
Road, London SW1V 2SA

ISBN 1 85958 493 4

Printed and bound in Guernsey by The Guernsey Press Co. Ltd

CONTENTS

PREFACE

IN ANY debate on the merits and demerits of corporal punishment, the real points at issue are often confused, distorted or unnoticed in the personal reaction of the debater to the offences or crimes for which fustigation is held to be a fitting punishment. Indignation or hatred, which often degenerates into fanaticism, outweighs every other factor. The inflaming or the development of the desire to punish results in the wish to maim or to crucify the individual responsible for the particular crime which has aroused hatred.

In no real or true examination of this subject of corporal punishment and all its connotative implications, can the historical, religious and anthropological aspects be ignored. A knowledge of the causes and effects of the various forms of flagellation which at one time enjoyed a great vogue in England and in other countries, contributes enormously towards a full understanding of corporal punishment in its relation to modern civilisation. In fact I would go further and say that without a searching examination of this historical background and its sociological and anthropological foundations any such understanding is impossible.

Now the story of flagellation, in any *complete* sense of the word, has never been written. To me, and I have no doubt to many others, this is a matter for some surprise. For this story in all its astounding and wellnigh incredible mixture of cruelty, eroticism, superstition, voluptuousness and persecution, exhibits a panorama of amazing interest. One's horror at the

9

cruelty and obscenity connected with the practice of flagellation, is overshadowed by one's amazement at its universality, its tolerance, and even its approval throughout the civilised world for, at least, eighteen hundred years of the Christian dispensation.

True enough, there are many books dealing with flagellation. A few, excellent as they are from a purely historical point of view, fail to present (largely through the fact that they were written many decades ago, when psychology was in its infancy) any adequate examination of the sociological and erotological aspects of the phenomenon, to link up its anthropological with its pathological connotations. Others are cumbrous, or fragmentary, or superficial. What is more, in most cases, attempts have been made to avoid offending the susceptibilities, or outraging the moralistic scruples, of Puritans, patriots and gobblers-up of the fairy-tales that so often pass for history; and, in consequence, these books are often little more than collections of anecdotes dealing with instances of spanking refractory children or religious fanatics. Others, again, are frankly pornographic, and are sold at ridiculously high prices by dealers in erotica.

In the main, therefore, the contributions which, in any truly comprehensive or exhaustive, as opposed to a purely historical, sense, elect to cover the ground, are not those publications dealing specifically with flagellation *per se*, but are to be found in general works on sexual psychology, pathology and psychoanalysis, such as those of Havelock Ellis, Freud, Féré, Krafft-Ebing, etc. And these are either not available to the general public, or are presented in a jargon which is largely meaningless to those unversed in the terminology employed in medico-legal and psychological literature.

It is only by linking up the psychological with the religious and so-called punitive aspects that the true and full significance of flagellation as a social phenomenon can be realised and analysed. Novalis truly says: "It is rather astonishing that the association of lust, religion and cruelty during all these years has not caused mankind to pay more attention to the intimate

character of their relationship and to their common aims."*
Cruelty and torture as sociological phenomena are continually changing. It is as true as it is amazing that neither the one nor the other is static. The custom which meets with unanimous approval in one generation may rank as the most reprehensible form of cruelty in the next. Moreover, punishment (whatever its precise form) that has the sanction of the law is rarely considered to be cruel in the State where it is practised. It rarely is denounced as torture. At one time the form of punishment adopted in the case of infanticide was to compel the parent responsible for the crime to live for a couple of days and nights with the child's dead body affixed to his or her neck, a method which today would be condemned and denounced as a reversion to barbarism. And yet I have known highly respectable individuals of both sexes who have adopted an analogous method in the case of a dog caught in the act of killing a fowl.

Cruelty is inherent in mankind. The growth of civilisation and the apparent coincident development of humanitarianism is extremely deceptive, giving rise to the idea that mankind in the mass is becoming more humane. What actually is happening is that a small section of society is succeeding in preventing, to a considerable extent, overt cruel acts on the part of the majority. *Every form of cruelty which the law allows is practised in a wholesale manner and with gusto by the public.* It requires the interference of the law with man's inherent cruelty as expressed in any specific direction, over an extended period of time, and the ranking of this specific act as a crime, to result in universal horror on the part of society as a whole at any manifestations of that particular form of cruelty or persecution. But this horror at and ostracism of any individual perpetrator of the crime is *expressly limited to the offence as defined by the law.* It does not extend to any analogous and equally cruel practice which, accidentally or otherwise, has escaped being pilloried as a crime.

This distinction between man's actual overt acts of cruelty

* Quoted by C. S. Féré, *Scientific and Esoteric Studies in Sexual Degeneration in Mankind and in Animals*, Anthropological Press, New York, 1932.

and his unlimited potential cruelty is a point of immense significance. It suggests the explanation for reversions to forms of barbaric cruelty by civilised races as exemplified in times of war and revolution.

The horror of most people of today at the idea of forcing human beings to work under the lash of the whip, as was customary in so many parts of the world at one time, is a sincere horror, and a return to the practice, *under existent social conditions*, would never be countenanced; but there is no horror experienced or understood at the idea of forcing a horse to work under the whip, a sight which can still be seen the whole world over even in these enlightened days. Only when the whipping of the horse-slave is ostracised as universally and as determinedly as is the whipping of the man-slave can it be truly said that society is beginning to realise what cruelty really implies and that any hope of its ultimate disappearance is conceivable.

There is a tendency to look upon flagellation as a dead subject, much as one looks upon the Greek and Latin tongues, on witchcraft, and on the cosmogony of the Book of Genesis; to consider its interest on a par with that of King Henry VIII's amours, or Queen Elizabeth's virginity, or the polygamy of the Mormons. It is true that the modern schoolboy has little practical acquaintance with the birch or the cane; it is true that penal floggings are, practically speaking, obsolete; it is true that ecclesiastical flagellation is a thing to laugh at. But it is not true that flagellation is actually defunct. It is not true that the psychological motivation behind flagellation is not in existence today, and liable to take form in some outward expression akin, at any rate so far as concerns its essential cruelty, to flagellation. It is not true that sadism and masochism are non-existent, or even in decline.

Quite the reverse, masochism, in its symbolic or psychological form, is increasing with the development of civilisation. Any extension of democracy is bound to lead to a corresponding increase in a sort of masochism on the one hand and of sadism on the other, in the forms of continually increasing submission to bureaucratic interference and to communal bullying. Years ago, Nietzsche, probing deeply into the motivations actuating society, discerned the existence of phenomena—which Schrenck-Notzing describes collectively as algolagnia*— underlying and imperilling so-called civilisation: the sadism behind, and functioning through, government, religion, law and order; the masochism readily observable in the meek and slave-like submission of the masses to continually increasing inroads upon their freedom, the ever-increasing subservience of man to the domination of woman.

True, it may seem at first glance a far cry from these seemingly harmless sociological manifestations to the sexual subservience which represents true masochism; but it must be remembered that once planted, the tree may develop along unorthodox lines. The modern child and the modern adult tend to depend more and more upon the State to act as their wet-nurse, their preceptor, and their guardian. Each year sees an increased tendency to leave things to the State and its ever-increasing army of officials; each year sees an increased tendency not only to submit to rules of conduct nailed up for the guidance of the people, but to approach these bureaucratic officials in a genuflective manner, humbly asking to be allowed to submit to them for guidance in matters where no ready-made rules are available. All these things are cumulatively destructive and dismaying. All point to the creation and development of precisely those attitudes of mind and conduct where an extension of true masochism may well develop in an increasingly feministic civilisation.

We see the growing tendency in these directions emphasised in much of the literature and the drama of today. The heroes and the heroines of popular fiction are often masochistic in behaviour as well as in outlook. In the plays of Bernard Shaw, in particular, male masochism is featured time after time.

The masochistic features of civilisation—and especially of present-day civilisation—are as far-reaching as they are ecu-

* Algolagnia is a term used by Schrenck-Notzing to include both sadism and masochism as being interlinked forms of painful lasciviousness.

13

menical. The possession of an 'inferiority complex', which, in modern society, is the self-apologetic mode (borrowed from the psycho-analysts) of describing what is perilously near to being an expression of masochism, is so popular as to be fashionable.

The gulf between the wilful self-imprisonment in cords of the schoolboy and the gleeful genuflexion of proletariat and aristocrat alike to the will of a dictator, is apparently a wide one. But in reality the basic roots of both phenomena are the same. Similarly, the self-same masochistic basis is at the root of the urge which leads men, gregarious even in their mental and moral perversities, to band themselves together in secret societies, clubs and clans: to prance bombinatingly as Elks, Kiwanis, Oddfellows, and so forth.

All these factors to which I have referred still, from place to place and from time to time, individually, collectively and cumulatively, exert considerable influence. Civilisation is unquestionably constantly threatened by masochism of a purely symbolic kind. Whether the tendency will be still further extended, or whether a strong reversal of attitude will ultimately set in, are questions which the future alone can decide.

Mob sadism is always existent in a latent form. It always exists surreptitiously. It functions continuously and universally in the form of the torture of animals. Given the slightest degree of legal approval, it functions in the shape of 'third-degree methods' in a good many countries. It blooms with a measure of barbarity rivalling the worst features of the 'Holy' Inquisition whenever war or revolution provides the incentive or the excuse, as in the world wars of 1914-18 and of 1939-45. It functions, always symbolically, in the murder trials which are headlined in the Press, in the cannibalistic rites which form the most spectacular features of the Christian religion.

All these matters and their intricate relations, the one to the other, I shall, in the following pages, endeavour to make clear. The examination of flagellation in its manifold forms, of its psychological background, and its correlations, will, I think, prove to be a study of the most profound significance, presenting a social document of intense interest and importance; and pointing to the need to abolish for ever a form of punishment so barbaric, so brutal, so degrading, so psychologically and physically dangerous, and so deficient in reformative, expiatory or reformative qualities.

The writing of the book has not proved by any means an easy task. The subject bristles with difficulties. It is not that there is any lack of material, any deficiency in evidence, for the finding. On the contrary, one of the major troubles is the existence of far too much of both. Selection of evidence from the vast available mass has presented a problem in itself. My aim has been to present just enough essential documentary material and, at the same time, to avoid making the book tedious or wearisome. Then, too, the sexual aspect, so essential to any clear understanding and adequate examination of the subject, has called for the deepest probing, and the ruthless facing of what to many may prove unpalatable facts. It would have been easy to ignore the sexual side and all its implications, as so many writers on the subject of corporal punishment have done before. But this ostrich-like attitude would have been not only to evade one of the main issues, but to present a distortion of the truth. One of the most pernicious features of corporal punishment lies in the possibility, on the one hand, of pandering to the sadistic element in mankind, and, on the other, of awakening or developing sexual libido. The flogging of children, in particular, is likely to be accompanied by unhealthy sexual excitation; and on this one ground alone ranks as a form of punishment out of tune with modern scientific reformative and educational trends.

I firmly believe that the book dealing with corporal punishment and its analogues, on the lines I have here advanced, fulfils a very present need, and this conviction on my part constitutes my justification for writing the book, and my solace for the search, during many months, into the customs and habits of that queer, amazing, barbaric, and often disgusting animal called man.

GEORGE RYLEY SCOTT.

15

PART ONE

THE PSYCHOLOGY OF FLAGELLATION

I: THE INHERENT CRUELTY OF MANKIND

MAN is cruel. He has always been cruel. He is cruel to everything which he considers inferior to himself. He is cruel to both his fellow men and to animals. The advance of civilisation has not resulted in man losing his capacity and appetite for cruelty; it has merely directed both into fresh channels, or camouflaged them, or temporarily subjugated them. The delight which man experiences in persecuting others shows itself today in various forms; and where physical persecution is impossible, psychological persecution takes its place. The fact that a barbaric act is practised under the aegis of justice, and the additional fact that it is conceived to be a fit punishment for the crime, do not alter or in any way mitigate its basic cruelty.

The savage discovered for himself the punishing element in pain. It was perhaps one of the first things that savage man did discover. Pain, he found out, whenever he himself experienced it, seared his brain with a lasting impression, an impression that persisted far longer and far more distinctly than did any other impression. It endured, for instance, much longer than did its opposite—the feeling of pleasure.

Unconsciously the savage, in his primitive thought-concepts based upon physical reactions, went beyond either morality or its religious correlations. The abstract concepts of good and evil, as we understand them, and as Christianity broadcast them through the mouthpiece of its anthropomorphic godhead, meant nothing at all to the savage. Did this factor confer upon him any benefit? Was that factor likely to injure him? The answer to

17

these simple questions constituted the basic reasons for the formulation of the savage's rules of conduct. He met with an enemy, and he promptly made every effort to exterminate that enemy. It was a case of exterminate or be exterminated. Crude philosophy, perhaps, baldly and bluntly expressed, but eminently sound. And in its ultimate analysis, morality as we understand it today, stripped of its trimmings, its rococo decorations, its fancy terminology, its euphemistic reasoning, differs little from this original, simple, crude definition.

Nietzsche, in his masterly analysis of civilisation and its origins, drew attention to the amorality of the savage. He showed how the punishments meted out to members of the tribe who transgressed its unwritten code were conditioned by exactly the same motives as were his own acts towards an enemy. In other words, the savage made no real distinction between an enemy of the tribe and an enemy of himself within that tribe. His instincts told him to destroy or to maim or to injure any human being or any animal which might conceivably injure himself. Because of this, in all primitive societies, punishment, observed and examined through humanitarian spectacles, is a barbarous procedure. Almost always does it involve mutilation or death, preceded by torture in some physical or psychological form.

Pain and suffering sear deeply; they engrave in indelible letters on the tablets of human memory. These constitute the lessons learned by savages. They constitute no less the lessons learned by civilised races. Man made pacts with his brethren; later he made promises to and covenants with his god. Punishment, or the fear of punishment, was the factor which made him remember to keep these promises and to observe the covenants.

Arising out of all this came the idea of sacrifice as a means of propitiating god. Every religious cult reeked, in its early forms at any rate, of sacrifices in some form or other. At first these sacrificial offerings took the shape of fruit and vegetables laid upon the altars; then came animals; finally and inevitably came human beings. Often, enemies captured in warfare, or strangers who were met with accidentally and captured, served to propitiate the gods. But these were not always available, and others had to be pressed into service. Slaves and criminals were frequently used. Children were commonly victims of sacrifice. Thus the Phoenicians gladly sacrificed their youngsters; according to Herodotus, the Egyptians often sacrificed the first-born of the family; in ancient Mexico and in Peru, every kind of human was sacrificed to the Sun-god; while, according to the Biblical texts, the sadistic god of the Hebrews tirelessly and ceaselessly called for burnt offerings of men, women, children and animals, as exemplified in the commands issued by Jehovah through his spokesman Moses in the twenty-seventh chapter of Leviticus.

Finally came Christianity with its concept of original sin; its persistent masochism; its idea of personal sacrifice; its self-inflicted torture, psychological and physical; reaching its apogee in the doctrine of atonement with the sacrifice of the Christ Jesus himself.

This idea of sacrificing human beings was a good deal mixed up with cannibalism. As it became evident that the god most assuredly did not eat the flesh of the slaughtered animal or human being, through the non-disappearance of the corpse, it was assumed that only the soul or spirit was consumed by the god, the actual flesh being left to be eaten by his devotees themselves.

From this arose the idea of consuming vicariously the flesh and blood of the god himself or of his representative, which persists to this day in the Eucharist.* Thus: "Except ye eat the flesh of the Son of man, and drink his blood, ye have no life in you."† Similar vicarious forms of sacrificial cannibalism were observed in rival contemporary religions as well as in pagan cults.

The whole Christian code of ethics was compiled in accord

* The Roman Catholic and the Greek Churches affirm the doctrine of transubstantiation, a reversion to the pagan anthropophagous belief that the wine and the bread are actually the blood and flesh of Christ.

† John vi. 53.

with these barbaric basic sacrificial ideas, grafted upon the savage concepts of good as something pleasurable or beneficial, and of evil as something painful or harmful. "All morality," thunders Nietzsche through the mouthpiece of Zarathustra, "is nothing more than an expression of expediency." In other words, morality is an unstable concept or collection of concepts, veering and teetering in weathercocky mutability, according to the will-to-power of autocracy expressing itself in ponderous and euphuistic despotic form or in hegemony camouflaged as democracy.

Cruelty, persecution, the humiliation of one's fellow men, are all expressions of the will-to-power functioning in every phase of animal and human life. It would appear to be natural for every man to grasp the opportunity of exhibiting his superiority over others, and nothing provides better and more spectacular evidence of this superiority than the trampling underfoot of one's fellow men, and especially of competitors and possible rivals. Success, as the world understands and worships it, is merely a manifestation of this will-to-power. Cruelty, physical or moral, is inseparable from its functioning. Even where man cannot himself shine as an individual despot, he grasps any opportunity that offers to take part in communal despotism, as exemplified in mass persecution. Hence his enthusiastic participation in the lynching of human beings, the hunting of animals, and the like; his hurrahing at every opportunity that is given him of hounding someone to death. On a lesser scale, the same basic motive actuates the individual taking part in a revivalist campaign. He is, for the time being, lifted out of the ordinary rut of life, he is in a position of authority, he is something of a hero in his own imagination if in no one else's, and the fact that in the process he tramples underfoot one or more of his fellow human beings matters not one jot.

The will-to-power explains much of the existent cruelty in the world apart from and in addition to any purely sadistic motive. It also explains much of the cruelty often attributed to religious or political enthusiasm. It explains much of the cruelty to which Richter refers in the following revealing passage:

20

"There lies in man a terrible cruelty; just as pity may be such as to cause him positive pain, so may the infliction of punishment amount for him to a sweet pleasure. It is a strange thing, proved by observing schoolmasters, soldiers, peasants, hunters, overseers of slaves and murderers, and also by the French Revolution, that cruelty incited by anger can easily become so inflamed as to be a source of enjoyment to those who inflict it, to whom the cry, the tear, and the bleeding wound are really a refreshing fountain to still their thirst for blood."*

Not only does the individual take pleasure in performing acts of cruelty himself, but he experiences similar pleasure in witnessing exhibitions of cruelty performed by others. It has been so from the beginning of time. The sacrifices to the gods among savage and primitive races are typical early forms of spectacular cruelty giving pleasure to those witnessing them. The sacrifices, first of animals and then of humans, were applauded by the populace; the roasting of the victims was accompanied with hoots of joy. So, too, the torturing of prisoners of war, the punishment of criminals.

The sports of all nations the world over since the dawn of civilisation provide evidence in all abundance of this delight in witnessing exhibitions of cruelty. In the Roman Empire at its mightiest we have the delight of emperors and aristocrats in seeing prisoners, criminals, slaves, and others, forced into filling the roles of gladiators, being torn to bits by wild animals, and, when the supply of humans ran short, of animal pitted against animal in a struggle to the death. An echo of this custom survives today in the bull-fights of Spain. Another echo survives in the fox-hunts of England.

But quite apart from extensive mistreatment of animals, the United Kingdom itself (and in this its record is probably no worse than any other country's) has a dismally disturbing history of cruelty to the young, as is amply testified by the annals of humanitarian organisations, especially the National Society for Prevention of Cruelty to Children.

* Jean-Paul Richter, *Levana*.

II: THE AMBIVALENCE OF PLEASURE AND PAIN

WE have seen that cruelty, if not actually instinctive in mankind, is fostered and developed from a very early age—certainly it is present in some form in the infant. We have seen that cruelty exists today, despite our boasted humanitarian civilisation. We have seen that, with the growth of civilisation, the crude, purely physical cruelty of the primitive man, while still existent, is to some extent displaced and overlaid by a psychological form of cruelty. We have seen how the cruelty of the individual may express itself either in an active or a passive form, and how, in the same individual the one form may be alternated with the other.

We see an example of the passive part played in the administration of pain, where the female delights in the thought that two males are fighting for her favours. In the animal world, the female looks on while two rival males fight for supremacy: she eagerly succumbs to the advances of the victor. In savage races, where marriage by capture is common, the process is little removed from the procedure among animals.

It is here that we see an analogy existent between the pursuit of the female animal by the male previous to the love embrace, and the pursuit which ends in conflict and death. In many cases this love pursuit and eventual capture is playful; in others the male is bent upon satisfying his lust irrespective of the desires or wishes of the female. In some savage races the male takes the woman he wants by brute force.

The sex act among animals is often in itself a painful procedure. Apart from and in addition to the painful nature of initial coital intromission, the love-play which precedes sexual intercourse is rarely devoid of roughness and injury. The male dog often bites the bitch before copulation; stallions bite mares; cockerels dig their beaks into the heads of the hens and inflict bodily injury with their spurs during the sex act; crabs perform mayhem; often the female spider bites off the male's head after coitus; the copulatory organs of many other animals, birds and insects unquestionably induce scarification and sometimes severe injury.

Even in humans, when it is remembered that sensation during coitus depends upon the degree of irritation between the penis and the vagina, the relation between pain and pleasure during the coital act will be apparent. The same degree of irritation applied to any except an erotogenous zone, and divorced from sexual excitation, would be nothing less than painful or un-pleasant. In this connexion, men and women—especially women—vary enormously in the degree of irritation which is necessary in order for them to secure pleasure from the sex act. The friction between the vagina and the glans penis which in one man is sufficient to cause ejaculation, in another will have little or no pleasurable effect, while in yet another instance it may cause soreness, with resultant inflammation. In the female, the vagaries of sexual stimulation resulting from clitoridean and vaginal irritation range all the way from the most volup-tuous feeling, manifesting itself in repeated orgasms, to com-parative anaesthesia on the one hand and vaginismus on the other. Many factors are responsible for these varied conditions, and they may be conditioned by all kinds of physical as well as psychological reasons. Among the more pronounced physio-logical causes are disproportion between the male organ and the female vagina, which may be present from the beginning of marriage, or which may manifest itself in later years as a result of successive parturitions widening the vaginal passage; or even through excessive or repeated intercourse.

In savage and primitive races, where libidinous desire and sensuality are not artificially checked, subdued or diverted, as they are in civilisation, the female makes no effort to conceal her disappointment if intercourse does not provide her with sufficient sexual excitation or pleasure; and from her point of view a semi-impotent male is one to jeer at and to spurn. It is these reactions of the female to sexual excitement, in combination with her own desires, that cause the male to devise various means for increasing the natural powers of irritation possessed by the male organ, and to endure pain and suffering in order to put these devices into practical effect. Hence the notorious *ampallang* used by the Dyaks of Borneo, for example.

Just as what, apart from sexual excitation, would unquestionably be considered painful, so also acts which in other circumstances would be considered to indicate anger or rage, in the throes of sexual excitement become indicative of love, and as such are not only tolerated but actually welcomed. Slaps and blows are accepted as caresses, scratches and bites form part of the love-play which is expected.

Apart from the specific connexion between irritation and pleasure in the act of coitus itself, pain is in certain circumstances a stimulant, just as hunger, fear, hate and other excitations are stimulants or depressives in relation to other coincident or existent concomitants. In an exhaustive study of the effects of the emotions upon somatic processes, Cannon points out that in pain and certain other emotions, the adrenal glands are stimulated to increased secretory power, pouring into the blood-stream additional supplies of adrenalin, a substance which possesses extraordinary restorative powers, enabling muscles, which, through fatigue, senility, or other causes, have become enfeebled or flaccid, to regain immediately a temporary rejuvenation or reinvigoration.* How pain, in the form of flagellation administered to certain parts of the body, may act specifically as a sexual stimulant we shall see at a later stage in this inquiry.

* W. B. Cannon, *Bodily Changes in Pain, Hunger, Fear and Rage*, Appleton, New York, 1929.

III: BASIC MOTIVES: CONSCIOUS AND UNCONSCIOUS

WHY should the causation of pain, humiliation and suffering in fellow humans and in animals arouse pleasure in the person administering these particular forms of cruelty? Why should the mere witnessing of some form of barbarity give pleasure to the spectator? These are deep and difficult problems. They are mixed up with so many other sociological and psychological factors that the solutions are neither easy nor straightforward.

We have seen that in savage and primitive races the idea of cruelty to prisoners, slaves, enemies, and others, arises through its value as a deterrent; we have seen how in civilised societies this basic idea was developed until an elaborate code of punishments was devised for dealing with various crimes and misdemeanours. The ostensible notion behind all torture or cruelty inflicted as a form of punishment, in civilised society at any rate, is one of justice. All the terrible and monstrous cruelties practised in the Christian era have been perpetrated in the blessed names of morality, humanity, divine justice. For the good of the people has been the battle cry of the persecutors and the justification of their acts. But is this explanation the true one? I very much doubt it.

There is an idea, maintained and perpetuated through the ages, that the judges, the persecutors, the executioners, and, in short, everyone who is in any way connected with the putting into operation of any form of punishment, is actuated by a stern and rigid sense of justice. It is a fiction. It is true that hostile historians are inclined to view these acts of justice through quite different lenses; but, at the time, and by their compatriots in power, justice is the motive which is held to actuate every such action.

Now, apart from the fact that law and justice are rarely synonymous, seeing that every law that has ever existed has been devised and given official sanction by individuals who are in some way interested in putting the law into operation, I cannot subscribe to the notion that every judge and every hangman have pursued their professions because they were intent upon seeing justice done and for no other reason. Even if, by some chance, they may originally have set out with some such purpose, a few months' experience would have sufficed to convince them that the idea was a myth and a delusion, and they would have given up their jobs in disgust and despair. One might just as well contend that the clergyman invariably selects his profession, and continues to practise it, in the sincere belief that he is plucking brands from the burning and sending souls to heaven with clean consciences and repentant minds.

If one wishes to get within measurable distance of the truth, it is well that one should throw overboard the notion that any such thing as pure unalloyed altruism exists. The good which anyone does is nearly always incidental, and, in a sense, is forced upon one as an inevitable concomitant of what one does for some purpose quite removed from this much-trumpeted but actually subsidiary act of goodness. Birds, by eating up the slugs, give beneficial aid to the farmer, but they do not, in consequence, preen themselves on the good work they are doing in the name of the Almighty. The farmer sounds their praises, but the moment the seeds have been planted, he puts up ridiculous images in an effort to scare away his one-time allies, and if he sees a solitary sparrow investigating this sacred territory he curses it to all eternity and promptly reaches for his gun. The cat kills mice, and there are those who hold that the good Lord made the animal for this special purpose; but with equal glee it kills, if it gets a chance, the canary and the chickens; pastimes these which the birds' owner is inclined to view rather differently. Similarly, the basic motives which lead

26

men and women, in the overwhelming main, to do this and to promote that, to combat evils, to institute reforms, have nothing whatever to do with the avowed objects. Any success which is achieved is, in reality, subsidiary to this main basic but hidden or obscured object.

Mainly, of course, the basic motive is the earning of one's living. In a civilisation where there are more persons seeking and requiring jobs than there are jobs for the getting, this basic motive is an all-powerful one. The majority have little choice in the precise manner in which they earn their means of subsistence; and similarly once they have selected or have been pitchforked into a profession or trade, they are compelled, willynilly, to continue in that profession or trade until they turn into dust or retire in a state of senility. It is for this reason that so many persons hate the jobs which secure for them their bread and butter. Indeed, this applies to probably ninety per cent of the workers of the world. Then there are those who hate their jobs, but pursue them with apparent gusto and sincerity, but for some reason other than the mere accumulation of wealth. They could, these few, earn a living in some other walk of life, or they may have enough money to dispense with working altogether, but for reasons which they take care not to parade to the world, such for instance as the itch for power, or for fame, or for opportunities for philandering, they wish to continue in the particular profession or business they have chosen.

It is difficult to imagine a hangman enjoying his work, or a prison-warder, or a policeman, or a butcher—unless, of course, he is a sadist. It is similarly difficult to imagine a tax-collector securing pleasure from his work of bleeding his fellow men— many of whom are ill able to pay the taxes demanded—in order to secure money for expenditure upon what, as he knows full well, are all too often senseless official extravagances. It is even more difficult to imagine a police court lawyer taking pleasure in a career in which he is often compelled to indulge in wholesale lying, hypocrisy and chicanery.

It is easy to confound justice with revenge. The man or the

27

woman who has suffered personal injury or loss through the action of another is genuinely anxious that the individual responsible should suffer a degree of punishment proportionate to the crime committed, either at his own retributive hands or at the hands of the law. In this case the motive which inspires the desire for suitable punishment to be meted out to the offender is not an impersonal love of justice but, on the contrary, it is a desire for purely personal revenge. In the majority of cases, when this personal account has been squared, the urge to punish, to injure, and to cause suffering, vanishes.

We may rule out, therefore, as being virtually non-existent, the idea of a love of justice, pure and unalloyed, as a motive for punishment; and we may set it down, so far as concerns the huge majority of those who are in a position to dispense cruelty in the name of justice, that the paramount motive actuating them is the earning of the means to exist. They are paid to administer justice, and they administer it in accordance with the code of laws approved or sanctioned by society, even if it is against their own personal inclinations. They do this in the sure knowledge that failure to discharge this duty will lead to dismissal, and, as a sop to their consciences, they trot out the fly-blown argument that if they don't do it someone else will.

These, as I say, constitute the majority. But there is a minority who *do* enjoy punishing their fellow men, or witnessing their punishment; just as there are individuals who enjoy being cruel to animals or watching their sufferings. These are the sadists and sexual perverts of civilisation. Many of these men and women secure employment in prisons, or in reformatories, or in slaughter-houses.

Allied somewhat to these perverts are those whose penchant for witnessing or the imagining of acts of cruelty takes a symbolical form—a form which is deeply entrenched in modern civilisation, as Nietzsche, in a memorable passage has noted. Thus:

"Almost everything that we call 'higher culture' is based upon the spiritualizing and intensifying of *cruelty*—this is my thesis; the 'wild beast' has not been slain at all, it lives, it flourishes, it has only been—transfigured. That which constitutes the painful delight of tragedy is cruelty; that which operates agreeably in so-called tragic sympathy, and at the basis even of everything sublime, up to the highest and most delicate thrills of metaphysics, obtains its sweetness solely from the intermingled ingredient of cruelty."*

Then there are the individuals, again in the minority, but to be found in every country, and, when considered collectively, running into a big and alarming number, who experience sexual pleasure and stimulation through being flagellated. Whipping and sex are so intimately connected that, apart from sadists and masochists who can experience sexual feeling only while giving or receiving punishment, there are many others, and particularly senescents, who find the stimulation induced by flagellation conducive to sexual excitement and potency.

Finally and importantly, there is a factor which has a special bearing upon any consideration of the question of relative cruelty, to wit, the insensitiveness and callousness as regards suffering, whether human or animal, which comes with familiarity. It is because of this factor that so often the judge, the executioner, the witnesses, and everyone else in any way connected with acts of torture, of cruelty, and of inhumanity, through sheer repetition, become not only increasingly heartless, but also, in so far as it lies within their power, *increasingly severe*. In this connexion the remarks of Major-General Charles J. Napier are well worth noting:

"It is to be observed that when men are charged with the infliction of any punishment (no matter how revolting it may be in its nature) they generally become desirous of adding to its severity: their minds grow hardened by seeing such punishments inflicted, and they erroneously believe that the bodies of their fellow creatures grow equally indurated. To

* Friedrich Nietzsche, *Beyond Good and Evil*, Foulis, 1909.

correct this horrible disposition to cruelty which seems inherent in our nature, reason must interfere, or the heart becomes steeled through the eyes."*

* Major-General Charles J. Napier, *Remarks on Military Law and the Punishment of Flogging*, London, 1837, p. 146.

IV: THE CURATIVE AND MEDICINAL VIRTUES OF PAIN

MEDICINE, quackery and superstition have always been inextricably mixed up. They are, despite scientific elaboration, a good deal mixed up even to this day. The medicinal discovery of one age, hailed with resounding hosannas, becomes the superstition of the next age, and the myth of the third age. Among savages the witch-doctor or medicine-man ranks as the doctor of the tribe. He is the licensed practitioner—the one point where he differs from the physician in civilised states is in holding his licence from God. But this does not alter the fact that in reality the primitive medicine-man is a quack; just as many licensed doctors of civilisation in reality are quacks.

Quackery as applied to medicine is largely the exaggeration of a single basic principle or remedy into something bearing no relation to the actual facts. The drug or the herb which will give relief in the case of slight pain, or will cure some trifling ailment, is magnified into a universal panacea. This is the essence of quackery. The basic principle applying in some distemper is exaggerated into applying in every other distemper. This again is incidental to quackery.

We have seen that pain, in certain circumstances, is a stimulant and a source of energy. We have seen that under the influence of pain and anger, man is capable of efforts far beyond those he can perform in the ordinary way. We know that a man injured even unto death, may at that very time make a final effort such as in any ordinary circumstances he would be quite incapable of. We know that precisely the same thing happens often enough in the case of animals.

Now as long ago as the days chronicled in the Bible, the ancients had stumbled on these basic facts—they had observed that pain, in certain circumstances, acted as a stimulant. And straightaway, in accordance with the usage of *homo sapiens* the whole world over and from the beginning of time until the present day, they proceeded to build upon this basis a whole farrago of exaggeration, myth and quackery. Because pain acted as a stimulus to greater effort, they proceeded to argue and to act upon the supposition that the infliction of pain would stimulate the physical and mental energies of all men and all women in all circumstances. Because a whack on the back sometimes acted as a remedy for choking; they argued that whacking over the stomach would cure constipation, that flagellation of a woman's posterior would help her in the delivery of a child; that scarification of the shoulders was a sovereign cure for eye diseases.

In addition to this general hypothesis, the stick itself was thought to be blessed with magic and esoteric powers. It was the symbol of power; more, it was the symbol of the phallus and, as such, an object for universal reverence and respect.

In primitive races many diseases were thought to be caused by evil spirits. In the Bible this is reiterated time and again. Flagellation was a common method of driving out these demons or evil spirits; so were various other types of punishment which caused pain. Thus in Mark we read:

"And when he was come out of the ship, immediately there met him out of the tombs a man with an unclean spirit, who had his dwelling among the tombs; and no man could bind him, no, not with chains: because that he had been often bound with fetters and chains, and the chains had been plucked asunder by him, and the fetters broken in pieces: neither could any man tame him. And always, night and day, he was in the mountains, and in the tombs, crying, and cutting himself with stones." (Mark v. 2-5.)

Similarly Asclepiades, Coelius Aurelianus, Titus, Rhases and Valescus advised whipping as a cure for insanity; and for centuries the belief found strong support in many quarters. The Romans were under the impression that whipping would cause women to conceive; and as, in those days, the bearing of a child was woman's ambition as well as her destiny, she welcomed the blows with something approaching glee. According to Virgil and his commentator, Servius, at the festival of Lupercalia, certain selected men, stripped of all clothing and armed with leather straps, danced about the streets beating with these straps every woman they came across. This is an example of a superstition which prevailed through the ages. Another is the notion prevalent among sailors of ancient days that whipping the passengers would prevent a storm. In the *Satyricon* of Petronius it is related how Encolpus and Giton were flagellated with this express purpose in view. Thus:

"It was resolved among the mariners, to give us each 40 stripes, in order to appease the tutelar deity of the ship. No time in consequence is lost; the furious mariners set upon us with cords in their hands, and endeavour to appease the Deity by the effusion of the meanest blood: as to me I received three lashes, which I endured with Spartan magnanimity."

Seneca made a general statement which influenced many early writers on diseases and their treatment. He said: "Medicine begins to have an effect on insensible bodies when they are so handled as to feel pain." Also he recommended whipping as a specific in the treatment of fever. Others followed in his tracks, and soon those afflicted with such widely divergent maladies as lockjaw and smallpox, rheumatism and bowel troubles, found themselves soundly flogged for their pains. According to Mercusialis, Galen was not alone in advising whipping as a means of inducing the putting on of flesh. Many physicians prescribed the same course, and for centuries slave-dealers were accustomed to flog their captives with the express purpose of increasing their plumpness and consequently their market value.

According to Kisch,* in Ancient Greece, it was customary for the woman who was not blessed with a child during the first years of her marriage to pay a visit to the Temple of Juno in Athens, there to be cured by one of the priests of Pan, of her sterility. To this end she was ordered to strip naked, prostrate herself belly downwards, in which position she was flagellated by the priest with a whip made of goat's hide. There can be little doubt that these priests of Pan had stumbled upon the fact that flagellation on the buttocks stimulated sexual appetite (cf. Chapter XVII).

Whipping was very often practised in the baths. Regnard says it was a custom in Bothnia for girls to beat the naked male bathers with twigs in order to open their pores and induce evacuation of the bowels. It is possible, of course, that the procedure might have the effect in some cases, but it is extremely likely that the real aim was a sexual one. It must be remembered that in those days all baths were in reality brothels.

In their contention that the whip provided a sure cure for falling in love, the ancient physicians and philosophers were on safer ground. Rhases, Coelius Aurelianus, Valescus de Taranta, and Guainerius, are all united in this belief. Its efficacy in cases of malingering, of idleness and of shamming is believable too.

Superstitions die hard, whether they are connected with religion or with medicine; and for this reason we should experience little surprise that many of these ideas, crude as they were, survived through the centuries. Bartholin, writing in 1669, says:

"Among the Insubres, as I have proved in my *Cento of Histories*, the dead foetus is extracted from the mother by compressing the belly strongly, or striking it with wooden or steel balls. I have observed that boys, and men too, have been cured of pissing in bed by whipping."†

* E. Heinrich Kisch, *The Sexual Life of Woman*, London, 1910.

† John Henry Meibomius, *A Treatise on the Use of Flogging in Medicine and Venery*. In *Nell in Bridewell* (now available in this series, Luxor Press 9s. 6d.) there is an account of the flogging of a boy for enuresis, in a German prison, in 1848.

As a remedy for sexual impotence in men and sterility in women flagellation enjoyed a great reputation during many centuries of the Christian dispensation. In these respects, Meibomius, as we shall see later, was a great believer in its powers; so, too, was the Abbé Boileau. Millingen, as comparatively recently as 1839, wrote at length on the virtues of flogging in the treatment of disease, upholding the theories of the ancients. He says:

"Flagellation draws the circulation from the centre of our system to its periphery. It has been known in a fit of ague to dispel the cold stage. Galen had observed that horse dealers were in the habit of bringing their horses into high condition by a moderate fustigation; and therefore recommended this practice to give *embonpoint* to the lean. Antonius Musa treated a sciatica of Octavianus Augustus by this process. Elidaeus Paduanus recommended flagellation or urtication when the eruption of exanthematic diseases is slow in its development. Thomas Campanella records the case of a gentleman whose bowels could not be relieved without his having been previously whipped. Irritation of the skin has been often observed to be productive of similar effects. The erotic irregularities of lepers is well authenticated; and various other cutaneous diseases, which procure the agreeable relief that scratching affords, have brought on the most pleasurable sensations. . . . The effect of flagellation may be easily referred to the powerful sympathy that exists between the nerves of the lower part of the spinal marrow and other organs."*

Actually, whatever tonic effects flagellation may have are dependent upon three factors: (1) the physiology of the patient, (2) the psychology of the patient, and (3) the intensity of the whipping. Generally speaking, it was realised that to be in any way beneficial—and this applies in the sexual sphere (cf. Chapter XVII) as well as the mental sphere—the flogging

* J. G. Millingen, *Curiosities of Medical Experience*, second revised edition, London, 1839, p. 315.

35

must be of a mild or clement nature and not of protracted duration. Where the punishment reaches any considerable degree of severity there can, in all but specific and pathological cases, be nothing but depression and ill-effects generally.

PART TWO

PENAL FLAGELLATION

V: WHIPPING OF THIEVES, PROSTITUTES, ETC.

THERE is no means of knowing when or where flogging as a form of punishment originated. It is much older than civilisation. It was probably universal among all primitive and savage races. Certainly, as far back as history goes, there are records which indicate its universality and popularity.

The Old Testament, which ranks as the greatest catalogue of acts of cruelty and persecution that a sadistic god ever revelled in, betrays all the evidence one needs of the widespread practice among the Hebrews and the Egyptians of whipping or flogging as a form of punishment for all manner of crimes and misdemeanours. According to the laws of Moses, up to forty strokes of the rod could be given, the exact number varying with the nature of the offence and the whim of the judge. Thus:

"If there be a controversy between men, and they come unto judgment, that the judges may judge them, then they shall justify the righteous, and condemn the wicked. And it shall be, if the wicked man be worthy to be beaten, that the judge shall cause him to lie down, and to be beaten before his face, according to his fault, by a certain number. Forty stripes he may give him, and not exceed: lest, if he should exceed, and beat him above these with many stripes, then thy brother should seem vile unto thee." (Deuteronomy xxv. 1-3.)

Why forty was fixed as the maximum number of strokes is not quite clear, as in all cases of whipping the strength of the arm behind the lash or the vigour displayed by the one who

37

wields the whip has far more bearing upon the severity of the punishment inflicted than has the precise number of strokes. In any case, forty strokes seems to have been a most severe punishment, and must have often resulted in terrible injuries and possibly death. According to contemporary accounts, the number of strokes actually given, where the full penalty was imposed, totalled thirty-nine, as a three-thonged whip of calf parchment was used, each stroke thus meaning three separate lashes. The whip used was in reality a formidable weapon, as the thongs were of unequal length, one, the longest, being capable of encircling the whole body and inflicting terrible injuries to the breast as well as the back.

It would appear that the whip was the favourite instrument of punishment for many minor crimes and defections. It is specifically mentioned as a punishment for the betrothed woman guilty of sexual misdemeanour.* There is, too, evidence that it was used for inflicting punishment on political and racial offenders, both by the Hebrews and their contemporaries.

The coming of Christianity, and the replacement of the sadistic savagery of Jehovah by the forgiving magnanimity of Christ, saw a diminution of cruelty, and for the most part such references to flogging, apart from voluntary flagellation, as occur in the New Testament refer to the persecutions to which the disciples and apostles of Jesus were continually subjected. Thus, when, through the intervention of Gamaliel, the lives of the Apostles were spared, they were beaten† as a punishment and a deterrent. Saint Paul, according to his own account, received the maximum Jewish punishment of thirty-nine strokes of the rod; even Christ himself, before his crucifixion, was beaten by the order of Pilate.‡ All these, and other similar incidents, provide evidence that the whip was used to inflict punishment for all minor crimes, and, as an added indignity

* Leviticus xix. 20.

† "And to him they agreed: and when they had called the apostles, and beaten them, they commanded that they should not speak in the name of Jesus, and let them go." (Acts v. 40.)

‡ "Then Pilate therefore took Jesus, and scourged him." (John xix. 1.)

and persecution, before the consummation of a major sentence. Jesus himself had recourse to the rod on at least one occasion. Thus:

"And the Jews' passover was at hand; and Jesus went up to Jerusalem, and found in the temple those that sold oxen and sheep and doves, and the changers of money sitting: and when he had made a scourge of small cords, he drove them all out of the temple, and the sheep, and the oxen; and poured out the changers' money, and overthrew the tables." (John ii. 13-15.)

It would appear that the whip, during the time of Jesus, was a favourite instrument of punishment and coercion among the Romans. This whipping business indeed had been reduced to something of an art, different types of whip being used for different offences. Thus a simple flat leather strap, known as the *ferula*, was indicated where the offence was a minor one requiring the slightest form of castigation. For more serious offences, a whip made of cord-like twisted thongs of parchment, well-designed to lacerate the flesh, and known as the *scutica*, was called into play. Finally, came the horsewhip-like *flagellum*, a ferocious affair made of thongs of ox-leather. From a reading of Horace's *Satires* it is apparent that the choice of the rod, and the number of strokes, were left to the judge; and the same writer indicates the fiendish cruelty and vindictiveness apparent in some of the sentences when he mentions that the floggings continued so long, and were so excessive, that the executioner himself had to desist from sheer exhaustion.

There was, however, then, as now, one law for the rich and influential, and another law for the poor and obscure. The powerful often escaped the rod altogether, and where they could not avoid it in any complete sense, its severity was often tempered. Thus, in punishing nobles for various misdemeanours, the executioners were instructed, in accordance with the arbitrary decree of Artaxerxes Longimanus that the clothing only of these distinguished delinquents should be whipped.

There is an amusing story told of the poet, Jean de Menny. For casting reflections upon the chastity of certain aristocratic ladies, he was arrested, tried, and as a punishment for his offence, it was ordained that he should be stripped naked and the noble ladies upon whose honour he had dared to cast aspersions should be allowed to wield the whip upon his nude body to their own satisfaction. De Menny asked of the queen, who had ordered the form his punishment should take, the granting of one favour before the whipping commenced, and this request she graciously allowed. With ironic humour, the poet asked that the greatest prostitute of them all should step out and strike the first blow. It seems almost superfluous to add that the first blow was never struck.

One of the most remarkable and significant features connected with penal flagellation was the severity of the punishment for the most trivial of offences. It was obviously so among the Hebrews, the Egyptians, and others mentioned in the Old Testament; it was certainly so among the Romans and other early races of civilisation; it was assuredly so in England, in France, in Germany, in Russia, in China, and in other countries throughout the centuries until comparatively recent times.

No better example of this is there for the seeking than the notorious Whipping Act which was added to the statute book during the reign of the eighth Henry, in 1530. It was designed specifically to put down vagrancy, and it provided that any vagrant detected in the act should be haled to the nearest town possessing a market-place "and there tied to the end of a cart naked, and beaten with whips throughout each market town, or other place, till the body shall be bloody by reason of such whipping". This brutal and sanguinary act remained in force for some fifty years. Then certain modifications were made. The cart-tail business was largely discontinued;* the nudity clause was abandoned. Thenceforth the culprit was allowed to wear some clothing, at any rate, and was tied to a post while the whipping was performed. It was at this time that whipping-

* Whipping at the cart's tail was not finally abolished in Great Britain until early in the nineteenth century. The last sentence of this nature to be executed was in 1822 on May 8th, when a rioter was whipped through the streets of Glasgow by the hangman.

posts were erected in pretty nearly all the towns and villages throughout England. Their number and popularity are indicated by the lines of the poet, John Taylor:

> In London, and within a mile, I ween,
> There are jails or prisons full eighteen,
> And sixty whipping-posts and stocks and cages.

Men and women were whipped unmercifully for such trivial offences as peddling, being drunk on a Sunday, and participating in a riot. A search of historical records reveals that in 1641, at Ecclesfield, the sum of fourpence was paid to a woman for whipping one Ellen Shaw, accused of felony; in 1680 a woman was whipped at Worcester; in 1690, at Durham, Eleanor Wilson, for being drunk on a Sunday, "was publicly whipped in the market-place, between the hours of eleven and twelve o'clock";* in 1759, according to the Worcester Corporation records, a fee of 2s. 6d. was paid for whipping Elizabeth Bradbury, but, says a correspondent in *Notes and Queries* (October 30th, 1852), this sum probably included "the cost of the hire of the cart, which was usually charged 1s. 6d. separately"; in 1699, there is an entry in the Burnham Church register which records the whipping of "Benjamin Smat, and his wife and three children, vagrant beggars".† According to the writer of the article on "Whipping" in the *Encyclopaedia Britannica* (eleventh edition) "at the quarter sessions in Devonshire at Easter 1598 it was ordered that the mothers of bastard children should be whipped, the reputed fathers suffering a like punishment". On the occasion of the trial of Lady Alice Kyteler for witchcraft, in 1325, one of her associates was whipped until she made a confession involving Lady Alice as well as herself. The town council of Great Staughton, Huntingdonshire, in 1690, authorised payment of the sum of 8s. 6d. for guarding and whipping a female lunatic; and in this same town's records some twenty years later appears the entry of a payment of 8d. to one Thomas Hawkins, "for whipping two people yt the

* William Andrews, *Old Time Punishments*, Hull, 1890, p. 156.
† *Ibid.*

41

smallpox". There is an element of humour, grim though it be, in this apparent belief in whipping as a universal panacea for ailments as well as misdemeanours; but there is no grain of humour discernible in the brutal directions issued by the notorious Judge Jeffreys to the executioner charged with the whipping of a woman upon whom this monster in human form had passed sentence: "Hangman, I charge you to pay particular attention to this lady. Scourge her soundly, man: scourge her till her blood runs down! It is Christmas, a cold time for madam to strip. See that you warm her shoulders thoroughly." And there was nothing but ferocious, relentless, sadistic cruelty of the most pronounced type to be observed in the sentence passed upon Floyde the Catholic for "irreverent observations", by the House of Lords, in the reign of James I—a sentence of life imprisonment, preceded by branding upon the forehead and whipping at the cart's tail from the Fleet to Westminster Hall. The following detailed account of this extraordinary affair is reprinted exactly as it appears in *The Percy Anecdotes* of 1820-3, under the heading of "Scandalizing a Princess":

"When the news arrived in England, that Prague was taken from the Palsgrave of Bohemia, who had married the Princess Elizabeth, Mr Edward Floyde, a Roman Catholic gentleman, who happened to be a prisoner at the time in the Fleet, was heard to remark that Goodman and Goody Palsgrave were now turned out of doors, and to make several other irreverent observations of the same kind. The expressions were reported abroad, and so sinful were they deemed, that both Houses of Parliament thought it necessary to take them under their serious consideration. Of the proceedings in the Upper House, the only record that remains is the sentence; but those of the Commons have been preserved for the edification of posterity. Witnesses were examined who proved the words, and that Floyde's countenance was in a very indecent degree joyful when he pronounced them. It was further proved that he was 'a pernicious papist' and a 'wicked fellow', so that, in short, the poor gentleman had nothing to say for himself against the charge of having joked at the misfortunes of such high folks as 'Goodman and Goody Palsgrave'. The crime being thus established, a very strange debate arose as to the punishment to be inflicted on this most heinous offender. Sir Robert Philips was of opinion that since his offence had been without limitation, his punishment might likewise be without proportion. 'He would have him ride with his face to a horse's tail from Westminster to the Tower, with a paper on his hat, wherein should be written, "A Popish wretch that hath maliciously scandalised his majesty's children," and that at the Tower he should be lodged in little ease, with as much pain as he shall be able to endure without loss or danger of life.' Sir Frances Seymour was for standing more 'on the privilege and power of the house. He would have him go from thence to the Tower at a cart's tail with his doublet off, his beads about his neck, and that he should have as many lashes as he hath beads.' Sir Edward Giles thought that besides being whipped, he should stand in the pillory. Sir Francis Darcy 'would have a hole burnt through his tongue, since that was the member that offended'. Sir Jeremy Horsey thought the tongue should be cut out altogether. Sir George Goring agreed with none of the merciful gentlemen who had preceded him. 'He would have his nose, ears, and tongue cut off; to be whipped at as many stages as he hath beads, and to ride to every stage with his face to the horse's tail, and the tail in his hand, and at every stage to swallow a bead; and thus to be whipped to the Tower, and there to be hanged.' Sir Joseph Jephson 'would have moved, that a committee might be appointed to consider of the heaviest punishments that had been spoken of; but because he perceived the house inclined to mercy, he would have him whipped more than twice as far', &c. The debate was adjourned without anything being definitely agreed on; and before it was resumed, the House of Lords being resolved to be something more than sharers in the honour of punishing 'so vile and undutiful a subject', objected to the power of punishment assumed by the Commons, as an invasion of their privileges. The Commons, after long and violent debates, were at last obliged, after inserting a protest in their journals, to give up the point; and Floyde was now left to the upper House, who, equally 'inclined to mercy', pronounced the following sentence: 1. That the said Edward Floyde shall be incapable to bear arms as a gentleman and that he shall be ever held an infamous person, and his testimony not be taken in any court or cause. 2. That on Monday next, in the morning, he shall be brought to Westminster Hall, and there set on horseback, with his face to the horse's tail, holding the tail in his hand, with papers on his head and breast declaring his offence, and so to ride to the pillory in Cheapside, and there to stand two hours on the pillory, and there to be branded with a letter K on his forehead. 3. To be whipped at a cart's tail, on the first day of the next term, from the Fleet to Westminster Hall, with papers on his head declaring his offence, and then to stand on the pillory there two hours. 4. That he shall be fined to the king in £5,000. 5. That he shall be imprisoned in Newgate during his life. This inhuman sentence was carried into execution, with the exception of the third branch of it, which was suspended on a motion of the Prince of Wales (Charles I) till the pleasure of the house should be known. It is worthy of notice too, that the only opposition that was made to these proceedings was by the king, who sent a message to the House of Commons, in which, after complimenting them for their great loyalty, he remarked with characteristic shrewdness, that 'out of too great a zeal comes heresy'; and added that the lawyers who were present at the debate were inexcusable."*

I have presented this report of the case, including the details of the debate in the House of Commons, because I greatly doubt if there is for the finding a more illustrative example of the severity and cruelty with which those chosen to administer justice have exercised and flagrantly abused their power.

Many other instances of ferocious whippings of men and women, both for political and other offences, besprinkle and

* *The Percy Anecdotes*, collected and edited by Rueben and Sholto Percy, 1820-3.

blacken English historical records. Rarely did any shred of excuse for human frailty seem to enter into the souls of those sitting in judgment. In the days of Charles II, however, the Duke of York did interpose in one such case—he saved Lady Sophia Lindsay from being publicly whipped through the streets of Edinburgh for the crime of assisting at the escape of the Earl of Argyle, her own father-in-law.

Perhaps one of the most brutal floggings on record was Jeffreys' sentence of Tutchin to seven years' imprisonment, during which he was to be whipped every year through every Dorsetshire town, a sentence which, it was computed, "amounted to a whipping once a fortnight for seven years". Then there was the whipping of Dangerfield all the way from Aldgate to Newgate, and with such ferocity that he succumbed some days later; there was the flogging of Titus Oates with a six-thonged whip, in accordance with another brutal sentence ordered by the aforementioned sadistic Judge Jeffreys, a flogging which was continued until the prisoner was unable to stand on his feet.

In certain instances, and especially as public feeling against the whipping of women began to be aroused, female floggings were inflicted in the confines of the prison or its grounds. Thus we find at Launceston, in 1792, a woman thief was ordered "to be stripped to the bare back, and privately whip'd until she be bloody", where at the same time and in the same court, a male thief was given a similar sentence, except that in his case the whipping was to take place "in the public street".* There was, however, no Government regulation respecting the corporal punishment of women taking place in private, this being left to the discretion of the local authorities concerned, and in many parts of the country publicly performed female floggings continued until the Act was passed which abolished the corporal punishment of women altogether.

In the early eighteen hundreds the Australian penal settlements were the scene of floggings of so severe a nature as to rival, for sheer savagery, the worst that were inflicted in

* *Notes and Queries*, Seventh series, Vol. X, August 30, 1890.

England during the sixteenth century, or in the Southern States of America during the days of slavery. George E. Boxall, author of the *History of the Australian Bushrangers*, writes in that work:

"It is said that there were two floggers in Sydney who were regarded as artists in their profession. These men performed together, the one being righthanded and the other left. They prided themselves on being able to flog a man without breaking the skin, and consequently there was no blood spilled. But the back of the flogged man is described as having been puffed up like 'blown veal'. The swelling 'shook like jelly', and the effects were felt for a much longer period than when the back was cut and scored as it generally was, for we are told that the ground in the Barrack Square in Sydney, all round where the triangles stood, was saturated with human blood, and the flogging places elsewhere must have been in the same condition."

No more convincing indication of the terrible nature of these whippings, and of the mortal terror of them with which many of the convicts were imbued, can be cited than the fact of these prisoners deliberately mutilating their limbs in order to avoid punishment. All the dreary way to Australia these convicts, men, women and boys, upon the most trifling of pretexts, were beaten within an inch of their lives; arrived in the penal settlements, they were whipped, hammered and tortured repeatedly. The following account gives a graphic picture of the methods in vogue, and, in addition, indicates the triviality of the offences for which such cruel punishments were devised and employed.

"Here are some entries from the official journal kept upon the island.* '1844. The convict Richard Henry received 200 lashes for insubordination, and for endeavouring to trump up a charge of unfairness in dealing with prisoners on the part of Warder McCluskey.' Earlier, on 5 Nov., 1842, 'James Macdonald sentenced to receive 100 lashes and to work for three months in irons; and James Elliott to seventy-five lashes

* Norfolk Island—one of the Australian penal settlements.

and 3 months in irons, for having been seen to associate with each other by signals, when silence was enjoined in the gang.' Another entry says: 'Thomas Downie was ordered to the dark cells for seven days, and to receive 200 lashes for insubordination and refusing to work.''*

In the United States of America whipping was a favourite seventeenth-century punishment for various offences, and both male and female culprits came under the lash. An entry in the *New York Gazette*, dated May 14, 1750, reads:

"Tuesday last one David Smith was convicted in the Mayor's court of Taking or Stealing Goods off a shop window in this City, and was sentenced to be whipped at the Cart's Tail round the Town and afterwards whipped at the Pillory, which sentence was accordingly executed on him."†

Helin Billington, in June 1636, "was whipped in Plymouth for slander";‡ in the same year, for theft, Roger Cornelisen was "scourged in public";§ and, in 1643, one Roger Scott was "severely whipped" for "repeated sleeping on the Lord's Day and for striking the person who wakened him".||

Whipping was always a favourite form of punishment in the Bridewells of England and of other countries. The name 'Bridewell', as a designation for a house of correction, was first applied to a penal workhouse in London situated near Saint Bride's Well and given to the city by King Edward VI in 1553, to be thenceforward known as the City Bridewell. It was intended, in the words of Bishop Ridley, "for the strumpet and idle person, for the rioter that consumeth all, and for the

* Sacheverell Sitwell, *Dance of the Quick and the Dead*, Faber & Faber, 1936, p. 381.

† Quoted by Alice Morse Earle in *Curious Punishments of Bygone Days*, London, 1896, p. 80.

‡ *Ibid.*, p. 79.

§ *Ibid.*, p. 79.

|| Quoted by Alice Morse Earle in *Curious Punishments of Bygone Days*, London, 1896, p. 74.

vagabond that will abide in no place". Under a painting of the King which hung in the workhouse, appeared the following:

> This Edward of fair memory the Sixt,
> In whom with greatness goodness was commixt,
> Gave this Bridewell, a palace in olden times,
> For a chastening house of vagrant crimes.

Young women and young men both who were sent to the Bridewell appear to have been flogged unmercifully upon the faintest of pretexts. They were stripped and whipped in the presence of the governors of the prison for offences against the regulations; they were flogged while at work in the prison on the slightest provocation and for the most trivial offences. Even so comparatively recently as the nineteenth century, in certain South German prisons, according to the revelations contained in *Lenchen im Zuchthause*,* young girls were whipped unmercifully on entering and leaving the prisons, and often these whippings were performed in public. The author describes how an unfortunate fifteen-year-old boy was fastened down upon the whipping-bench, and with birches specially prepared for the purpose by steeping for hours in water, was thrashed on his naked backside until the blood coursed down his legs. And all this terrible punishment was imposed, not for any crime, not for any misdemeanour, not even for the breaking of a rule or a regulation, but because of an infliction calling for medical treatment and sympathy, to wit, bed-wetting in the night resulting from incontinence of urine.

Many of the girls and women who were sent to the Bridewells for correction were street-walkers, and part of the punishment meted out to them was whipping with the birch-rod in the presence of the governors of the prisons, and of such members of the public as were able, by influence or bribery, to obtain admission. For, strange as it may seem, the witnessing of flagellation was looked upon as an entertainment, and as

* This remarkable work dealing with penal flagellation was originally published in an English translation in 1900 by Charles Carrington of Paris under the title of *Nell in Bridewell*. It is now available in this same Luxor Press series, at 9s. 6d.

48

such was popular among the society ladies of the day—these 'bright young things' made up parties to go and see the delinquents whipped, much as today they might go to see a boxing match. According to Ned Ward in *The London Spy*, in the Bridewells, prisoners of both sexes were stripped to the skin and whipped in the presence of the Court of Governors.

Many graphic accounts of whippings in Bridewells besprinkle literature. In his work, *Life of Colonel Jack*, Daniel Defoe describes, through the mouthpiece of one of his characters, the whipping inflicted upon the leader (a mere youth himself) of a gang which had been engaged in kidnapping children. He was whipped until he "stamped and danced and roared out like a mad boy". The narrator goes on to say:

"I must confess I was frightened almost to death; for though I could not come near enough, being but a poor boy, to see how he was handled, yet I saw him afterwards with his back all wealed with the lashes, and in several places bloody, and I thought I should have died with the sight of it; but I grew better acquainted with these things afterwards. I did what I could to comfort the poor captain when I got leave to come to him. But the worst was not over for him, for he was to have two more such whippings before they had done with him; and, indeed they scourged him so severely that they made him sick of the kidnapping trade for a great while."

But, of all descriptions of the terrible and inhuman cruelty administered to boys and girls in the name of justice, none can surpass those contained in Reinhard's already mentioned *Lenchen im Zuchthause* or, to give the book its English title, *Nell in Bridewell*.* One of these accounts deals with the birching of a fourteen-year-old girl named Mina by the task-mistress, Cunigund. The girl, stretched on the whipping-bench, held down by an assistant, and with her clothes raised to expose her naked flesh, was whipped on her posterior and thighs until the skin split, the blood ran, and the child's screams reverberated through the building. But the governor gave no sign for the

* Available in this series, Luxor Press, 9s. 6d.

cruelty to stop. On the contrary, the fustigation continued until a second birch was broken up in the process.

The two most widely employed scourges in the Bridewells were the bull's pizzle and the birch. The bull's pizzle, elastic and capable of standing enormous strain, in truth a terrible weapon, was reserved for the more severe castigations. In a strong man's hand it was not only deadly in its punishing powers but dangerous to life and limb, and care had to be taken to avoid striking the seat-bone or lower end of the spine (*os coccygis*). On all ordinary occasions, the birch was the instrument selected. This was really a bundle of selected birch twigs, bound together at one end and fixed to a handle. The more fiendish of the flagellators, the day before the whipping was to take place, steeped the birch in vinegar and salt, a process which increased considerably the pain incident to the flogging.

The whip was for centuries a favourite means of castigating prostitutes. Mohammed, in the Koran, prescribes a hundred strokes with the whip as a punishment for both a whore and a whoremonger. In the French venereal hospital prisons of Bicêtre and Salpétrière, the afflicted women were scourged on entering, again on leaving, and on many occasions during their incarceration. At one time, procuresses in France, when detected and arrested, were mounted upon asses and, bearing inscriptions on their backs telling the tale of their guilt, were whipped through the streets *en route* for the prison. In Italy, prostitutes were branded and whipped; in Spain they were stripped naked and lashed with the birch; in Germany, at the time of Charlemagne, any man found with a prostitute was forced to carry her on his shoulders to the whipping-bench. These measures, however, like all attempts to suppress or to punish prostitution, were fortuitous, spasmodic, and to a certain extent half-hearted; and they were sandwiched between periods, often of long duration, when prostitution was tolerated and, on occasion, approved or glorified.*

* For the full story of the vain efforts to suppress prostitution, of its regulation, its ebb and flow, see my work, *Ladies of Vice*, Luxor Press, 9s. 6d.

In Brantôme's *Mémoires* there is an account of the whipping of Mademoiselle de Limeuil, who was a member of the French Court and Maid of Honour to the Queen, for writing satirical verse. The same authority tells us of the flagellation of Legat, the Spanish Court buffoon, because of certain remarks in questionable taste which he made in the presence of the Queen. In no country in the world was whipping so widely practised, so savagely and so vindictively inflicted, as in the Russia of the Czars. It was in Russia that was first used the terrible knout, a wooden-handled whip usually consisting of several thongs of raw hide twisted together and terminating in a single strand projecting some eighteen inches farther than the body of the knout. Variations were many, and were devised in accordance with the cruel whims of the executioners. In some cases wire was plaited with the hide; in others rings and hooks were attached to the ends of the thongs; in yet other instances the barbaric sadism of the individual wielding the whip caused him to harden the raw hide by dipping in water or other liquid and allowing it to freeze. Another form of whip much used in Russia was known as the *pleti*, consisting of three thongs of raw hide, to each of which was attached a leaden ball. It was introduced by the Emperor Nicholas as a substitute for the knout; but it is probable that both the *pleti* and the knout were employed indiscriminately.* In the reign of Peter the Great the maximum punishment was fixed at one hundred and one lashes with the knout, a whipping so severe that not even the strongest man could live through it. In fact, in very many cases and for certain crimes, the victims were actually whipped to death. The executioner, who had to serve an apprenticeship to his grisly and ghastly trade, armed with his terrible weapon could cause death either immediately by dislocation of the neck, or within a few days as a result of frightful injuries to the chest

* Although of Russian origin (fifteenth century) and usually associated with the Russian code of punishment, the knout was used in France and in other European countries after Napoleon's Russian campaign of 1814. Until 1845 it continued to be in general use in Russia. After that date both the knout and the *pleti* were reserved for use in the Siberian penal settlements.

51

and the intestines. Nor was the lashing with the knout confined to male prisoners. Women, too, were sentenced to this ghastly infamy and punishment. The story of Madame Lapuchin will bear repetition as providing a striking instance of revolting cruelty masquerading as justice, and to a woman at that.

This lady, cultured and beautiful, was one of the Court of Elizabeth, and was involved in the trial of a foreign ambassador for treason. Along with the actual conspirators she was sentenced to exile, preceded by whipping. In the presence of a huge crowd of onlookers, the beautiful Madame Lapuchin was stripped to the waist, whipped with the fearful knout until every inch of her body, from the waist upwards, was stripped of its skin and left bruised and bleeding. Lastly, her tongue was cut out, and she was sent to Siberia, as was the lot of so many creatures of fate in the Russia of those days. Miraculously, she escaped death.

Many famous men and women were knouted to death for real or fancied conspiracy. It was the common fate of nihilists and anarchists detected by the police or government spies. Then there was the Empress Eudoxia, condemned to whipping, imprisonment and deprivation of her riches, because of suspected infidelity. There was the poet Pushkin, who was whipped in accordance with the command of the Czar. There was Peter the Great's son, knouted to death, it was said, by his own father.

Of all the civilised nations, Russia may be considered to be the one which not only used the whip unmercifully, but also as the nation which continued to use it longer by far and for a greater variety of crimes than did any other.

The following eye-witness's account of the knouting of a man and a woman makes sorry reading:

"When the philanthropic Howard was in Petersburg, he saw two criminals, a man and a woman, suffer the punishment of the knout. They were conducted from prison by about fifteen hussars and ten soldiers. When they had arrived at the place of punishment, the hussars formed themselves into a ring round the whipping-post; the drum beat a minute or two, and then some prayers were repeated, the populace taking off their hats. The woman was first taken, and after being roughly stripped to the waist, her hands and feet were bound with cords to a post made for the purpose. A servant attended the executioner and both were stout men. The servant first marked his ground, and struck the woman five times on the back; every stroke seemed to penetrate deep into her flesh; but his master thinking him too gentle, pushed him aside, took his place, and gave all the remaining strokes himself, which were evidently more severe. The woman received twenty-five blows, and the man sixty. 'I' (continues Mr Howard) 'pressed through the hussars, and counted the numbers as they were chalked on a board for the purpose. Both the criminals seemed but just alive, especially the man, who had yet strength enough remaining to receive a small present with some signs of gratitude. I saw the woman in a very weak condition some days after, but could not find the man any more.' "*

Next to Russia, for sheer love of whipping, comes China, and little less formidable than the Russian knout is the Chinese rod of split bamboo. The sharp edges of the bamboo cut into the flesh, inflicting terrible lacerations. Little wonder that deaths, as a result of these floggings, have been frequent, and that those who escape this fate are often so terribly mutilated that they remain cripples for the rest of their lives.

The stick, too, was employed in other countries besides China; and was often used as an alternative form of punishment, or for certain specific offences, in countries where the use of the whip was customary. In some cases, especially where a stick or bastinado formed the instrument of punishment, the buttocks were not the selected points for battery. Thus, in Turkey, the soles of the naked feet were beaten with a stick.

With the development of civilisation, a more humane spirit began to show itself, particularly in regard to women. In 1817 the last recorded instance in Great Britain of whipping a woman in public occurred in Scotland. The young woman's crime was

* *The Percy Anecdotes*, 1820-3.

of no more heinous a nature than drunkenness and misbehaviour. For her pains, she was whipped through the streets of Inverness on three separate occasions. It was in this very year that the whipping of females in public was abolished by Act of Parliament.* This was followed, in 1820, by the Whipping of Female Offenders Abolition Act, which prohibited flogging of women either privately or publicly. It was under this English Act that James Miles, master of the Hoo Union Workhouse, was, in 1841, prosecuted and dismissed from his post on the grounds of whipping girls who were inmates of the workhouse.

In France, the whipping of the Comtesse de la Motte, for the theft of a diamond necklace, seems to be the last recorded instance of the public flagellation of a woman. The beautiful countess, with a halter round her neck, stripped to the skin, and secured to a cart, was whipped, branded on the shoulders with the letter V, and sent to the prison of Salpétrière.

Up to at any rate 1899 whipping appears to have been a common form of punishment in certain American prisons. According to the testimony of Al Jennings, gunman and train-robber, who was a prisoner in the Ohio State Penitentiary at the same time as William Sidney Porter, who was later to earn undying fame in the world of literature under the name of O. Henry, men were "whipped into bleeding insensibility" for certain 'crimes' against the prison regulations. This, the most dreaded of all forms of punishment, was known as 'seventy-five', and Jennings testifies to a prisoner having died under such a beating. The victim, bound hand and foot, was secured across a trough and flogged with razor-edged 'paddles' until, with his flesh hanging in ribbons and lacerated to the very bones, he became a mere lump of bleeding and unconscious flesh.

* A contributor to *Notes and Queries* (October 21, 1882, p. 338) states that he "witnessed a woman whipped at a cart's tail through the streets of the City of London as late as 1811. The procession passed along Fleet Street and under Temple Bar, halting at the broad expanse of road and open space at the east end of St Clement's Church, where the punishment ended."

In many American convict camps flogging was a customary form of punishment until the flood of public indignation succeeded in putting an end to it. In an article published in *Survey*, May 15, 1915, W. D. Saunders gives a heart-rending picture of the conditions revealed during an investigation concerning the convict camp in Pasquotank County, North Carolina.

"Convicts were whipped with a leather strap eighteen inches long, two inches wide and half an inch thick; this strap being fastened to a hickory stick two feet long. One method of whipping a convict was to stretch him between two trees and bare his back. One of the guards would wrap a heavy blanket about the victim's head and hold him to smother his cries. Another guard plied the lash. Many convicts thus whipped will carry marks for life."*

The 'convict lease system', which for so many years remained in force in the State of Georgia, was the cause of terrible cruelty. The system was originated after the Civil War by General Ruger, the provisional governor of the State. The convicts were hired out or 'sold' to speculators, who re-sold them to employers of labour. Mainly through the efforts of Fred L. Seely, editor of the Atlanta *Georgian*, public opinion compelled the authorities to conduct an official investigation into the whole system. At this investigation

"A number of witnesses told of having seen prisoners whipped to death. Every camp of Georgia convicts has a whipping boss who is required to keep a 'whipping register'—a book in which each castigation is recorded. It was brought out at the investigation that it was customary for the whipping boss to 'sand' his leather thong in order to make it 'sting'. Goode, a guard, sanded his leather strap to whip 'Abe' Winn, a white boy sixteen years old, sent up for stealing two cans of potted ham. 'Abe' was described by witnesses as 'a frail little fellow'. He had spilt hot coffee on the back of pigs owned by the guard.

* Quoted in *Prison Reform*, p. 232.

55

Goode had four negroes hold the boy while he delivered fifty-seven licks with his sanded strap. 'I saw him stagger to the hospital steps,' said one witness, Lewis, son of a former member of the Legislature. 'He could not lie on his back but died on his stomach. They said he died of consumption.' "*

Flagellation as a form of judicial punishment was comparatively rarely employed in Great Britain in the years immediately prior to the Criminal Justice Act, 1948, and only in certain cases, where it was felt that the most severe form of corporal punishment was merited, was a prisoner sentenced to flogging with the dreaded cat-o'-nine-tails. The 'cat' was never employed latterly where the offender was under eighteen.

In English law, certain of the cases where the 'cat' was used were those concerned with breaches of prison discipline, and especially offences in which personal violence was offered to the prison officials or for mutinous conduct. Any such case was tried before a special board of visiting magistrates, and the sentence was then confirmed by the Home Office. Corporal punishment in prison in England was finally abolished only as recently as 1967, under the Criminal Justice Act of that year.

The type of 'cat' used had nine tails made of whipcord. The tails were not knotted as they were formerly, but were 'whipped' with silk thread at their ends in order to prevent fraying. The flogging was across the bare back, not the buttocks. The kidneys and the neck were protected by means of leather bands. A doctor was present, who had the power to stop the flogging at any moment. In England the head of the prisoner was screened so that he could not see the officer who was wielding the 'cat'; in Scotland this did not apply.

Flogging might also be ordered for robbery with violence;† where the offender was deemed to be an 'incorrigible rogue';‡

---

* Quoted in *Prison Reform*, from an article by A. C. Newell, in *World's Work*, October, 1908.

† These cases came under the Act of 1863, which did not apply to Scotland. There was no flogging of adults for theft in Scotland.

‡ Vagrancy Act of 1824.

for attempts to injure or alarm the sovereign by the discharge of firearms or the use of other weapons, and for certain offences against morality of which 'white slave trafficking', male solicitation and indecent exposure were the most common.*

In reply to a question in Parliament, the Home Secretary stated that during the year 1933 the number of persons ordered to undergo corporal punishment was forty-nine,† in five of the instances for offences against prison discipline.

The Secretary of State for Dominion Affairs, in reply to a question in the House of Commons, said that the number of sentences of whipping imposed during each of the years 1931 to 1935, in the District Courts of Southern Rhodesia, were: 1931, 418; 1932, 511; 1933, 676; 1934, 638; 1935, 722.‡ It will be noted that the figures showed a rising tendency.

In the decade covered by the years 1904-13 the number of men sentenced to undergo corporal punishment in England and Wales by Courts of Assize and quarter sessions was 61 out of the 1,414 convictions of robbery with violence; while in the decade 1926-35 there were 235 sentences involving flogging out of a total of 656 convictions.

Prior to 1948 the birch-rod might still be used, subject to certain restrictions, in the case of young offenders,§ magistrates being authorised to order the infliction of six strokes for anyone between eight and sixteen years. The punishment took place in a private room. After the police surgeon had made his routine examination of the boy, the object of this examination being to ascertain if a whipping would endanger life, the youngster was stripped, tied hand and foot to a tripod, and was then ready

* These cases came under the Vagrancy Act of 1898; and the Criminal Law Amendment (White Slave Traffic) Act of 1912.

† Out of a total of 49 floggings, 42 were for robbery with violence or assaults with intent to rob.

‡ *House of Commons Reports*, July 28, 1937. These figures relate to floggings inflicted upon both white and black subjects. There were no figures available showing the proportion of each race.

§ Birching is even now sometimes ordered in the Channel Islands and the Isle of Man.

for the infliction of the punishment.* The old-fashioned birch-rod of our grandfathers' days, sometimes soaked in water to make it more supple, was still used. The police surgeon re-examined the boy after each stroke of the birch, and gave any treatment that might be necessary at the end of the whipping. Usually a police constable wielded the rod, the parent or guardian having the right to be present at the whipping,† but in some cases the court allowed the father to carry out the prescribed sentence in the presence of a constable.

The figures for birchings ordered by Courts of Summary Jurisdiction, of boys under fourteen, given in the Home Office Report, show that whereas in 1912 there were about 2,000 cases, in 1916 and 1917 the numbers rose to 4,000 and 5,000, but after 1920 the figures rapidly declined. In 1935, for instance, there were 218 birchings. Of 13,248 boys under fourteen found guilty of indictable offences, 218 were ordered to be birched, this being attributed to their happening to come before one or other of the few courts which still had recourse to this method of correction.

The significance of this final statement must not be over-looked. It indicates plainly the unfairness manifest in a punitive system which allowed the imposition of so degrading and de-basing a form of punishment as birching to depend upon the personal whims of local magistrates. The question of whether a child culprit got a flogging was governed not by the nature of the offence against law or morality which he had committed, but by the rulings in force in the town or district in which he happened to live.

Many judges and magistrates ordered the 'cat' and the birch *whenever and wherever the law allowed them to do so*, and there can be little doubt that *floggings and birchings would have been much more common had the number of offences for which they could be given been increased.*

* The procedure varied in different districts. In some cases the boy was held in position over a bench or table while the birching was inflicted. In all cases the whipping was on the bare buttocks.

† The right of the parent to be present did not apply in Scotland.

In a single generation during the present century some barbarous sentences were given. Thus in 1909 a sixty-five-year-old man was sentenced at the Middlesex Sessions to "twelve strokes of the lash for begging and being an incorrigible rogue". This sentence was remitted by the Home Secretary, Mr Herbert Gladstone, and led to his stating in the House of Commons, on May 18th of that year: "If sentences such as this one became numerous, an occasion for legislation will arise."*

At the Leicester Quarter Sessions in 1936, a fifteen-year-old boy was sentenced by Mr Paul E. Sandlands, K.C., the Recorder of Leicester, to twelve strokes of the birch for housebreaking. According to the *Daily Mail* (January 15, 1936) the police were "a little worried at finding themselves the executioners of such a sentence, for there had not been a flogging in Leicester for more than twenty years, and they do not possess such a thing as a birch! The case," added the *Daily Mail*, "has raised a storm of indignation locally."

The following year, Mr Justice Lewis, at Manchester Assizes, sentenced Albert Henry Simons, for "robbery with violence", to nine months' imprisonment and twelve strokes of the 'cat'.†

In Oxfordshire, at Woodstock, a fortnight later, a "gypsy boy, aged 12, was ordered six strokes of the birch for setting fire to Woodstock Institution piggeries".‡

At Hamilton, in Canada, on May 22, 1937, Magistrate James McKay "sentenced Leonard Mancini to one month in jail and five strokes of the strap for assaulting his wife".§ In the same court, on May 27th, "charged with acting in a grossly indecent manner in a barn on Barton Street, J. Hawkey, no address, was sentenced to one year definite and six months indeterminate in the Ontario reformatory, and to receive eight strokes in the second month of his imprisonment".‖

* Quoted by Henry S. Salt in *The Flogging Craze*, Allen & Unwin, 1916, p. 70.
† *Daily Telegraph*, June 30, 1937.
‡ *Daily Sketch*, July 14, 1937.
§ *Toronto Star*, May 22, 1937.
‖ *Ibid.*, May 27, 1937.

VI: WHIPPING OF SLAVES AND SERVANTS

As I have already mentioned, it is one thing to beat or to whip a man with the express object of deterring him from the repetition of acts of gross cruelty; it is quite another thing to flog him to death or to cripple him for life as a punishment for petty offences or derelictions.

Civilisation has much to answer for. Its history is punctuated with the most horrible and most revolting cruelties that the mind of man can conceive. In no form has mankind's penchant for persecution shown itself more flagrantly than in the treatment of those of its kind whom circumstances have placed totally within its power, beyond hope of rebellion, resistance or escape. The treatment meted out to slaves, since the days of the Romans to within the memory of the living, will remain for all time a damning indictment of Christianity and paganism alike; an ineradicable blot upon the history of so-called civilisation.

The writings of Horace, Plautus, Juvenal, Petronius, Terence, Ovid, Martial and others, all provide testimony most abundant as to the universality with which the aristocracy of the Roman Empire flagellated their slaves. So much so was this the case that the whip itself became the emblem of slavery. The owner of a slave was vested with the power that goes with absolute possession. He owned the slave body and soul. The human creature ranked with the horse, the cow, or the dog, to be kicked and beaten at the whim of its master. Slave he was from birth to death. He was whipped for any and every crime or misdemeanour; he was whipped for the sins of omission as well as commission; he was whipped often enough to provide amusement for his master's guests. Frequently, very frequently, the slave died, either under the whip, or as a direct result of the punishment inflicted. For there would appear to have been no limit to the fiendish cruelty of the Roman aristocracy. They exercised their brains in devising means of intensifying the severity of the whippings. Not content with the scarification inflicted by the terrible *flagellum*, to the leather thongs they tied nails, bones and leaden weights.

Nor were these cruel practices confined to the masters of the slaves. Mistresses were not one whit behind in the frequency or the extent of the punishments they inflicted or caused to be inflicted upon the girl slaves who served them. Indeed, if anything, the fair ladies of the Roman Empire exceeded their brethren in the ingenuity they displayed in inventing trivial excuses for subjecting their serving-women to excruciating punishments. In many cases the anger resulting from personal disappointments, or occasioned by fancied slights, found its outlet in the subjection of the serving-maids to punishment and degradation. Almost every lady's boudoir, like the judicial chamber of the court, was decorated with an array of whips and other devices for punishment and torture; and so strongly anticipated was the inevitability of punishment that in some instances the serving-maids were compelled to strip themselves naked before attending to their mistresses' wants so that they were actually ready for immediate scourging in accordance with the whims of these tyrannical ladies. Even neglect on the part of their husbands was sometimes the cause of a slave-girl being soundly flogged. It was habits of this nature which induced Juvenal's satirical comment:

> For if overnight the husband had been slack,
> Or counterfeited sleep, or turn'd his back,
> Next day, be sure, the servants go to wrack.

In most instances the flogging was done by a male slave. But sometimes it was done by the public flagellator. In both cases it was a terrible punishment for the poor wretch whose lot it was to suffer. If her mistress happened to be in an especially cruel mood, the flogging continued until the lady was pleased to stop it. Occasionally she wielded the rod herself; and it was one of these aristocratic ladies who was the subject of Ovid's satirical verse:

> I hate a vixen that her maid assails,
> And scratches with her bodkin or her nails;
> While the poor girl on blood or tears must mourn,
> And her heart curses what her hands adorn.

This whipping of female slaves by their mistresses, on the slightest of pretexts, was undoubtedly due to motives other than a pure desire to punish, as will be apparent when we come to trace the connexion between sex and whipping. At any rate it reached such a pitch of severity and of universality that it became necessary for the Church to put its foot down. The Council of Elvira issued the following ordinance:

"If a mistress, in a fit of anger and madness, shall lash her female slave, or cause her to be lashed, in such a manner that she expires before the third day, by reason of the torture she has undergone; inasmuch as it is doubtful whether it has designedly happened, or by chance; if it has designedly happened, the mistress shall be excommunicated for seven years; if by chance, she shall be excommunicated for five years only; though, if she fall into sickness, she may receive the communion."

The very necessity to pass such an ordinance is all the evidence one needs respecting the sufferings to which these slaves must have been subjected. The fact that a religious body, while continuing to approve of thrashing within an inch of one's life, and the inflicting of anything in the way of injuries and mutilations short of death itself, considers it advisable to check the punitive excesses of its female members, provides a most striking commentary on the cruelty of its day. The male slaves and their masters are not mentioned in this precious ordinance.

Presumably Christianity in those days was well content for slaves of the stronger sex to be beaten to death.

Bearing some analogy to this ancient custom of whipping slaves, was the practice of whipping servants which, according to the accounts of contemporary historians, was at one time commonly indulged in by the English nobility. These servants were not, of course, slaves in the true sense of that term, seeing that they were not the actual property of their masters and mistresses, but their conditions of service were, in reality, little removed from slavery, and they were whipped for the most trivial offences. Thus, Lady Frances Pennoyer of Bullingham Court, Herefordshire, writing in her Diary for 1759-60, mentions the necessity to whip a new servant-girl for not being "nearly respectful enough in her demeanour". She describes the actual whipping thus:

"Dearlove, my maid, came to my room as I bade her. I bade her fetch the rod from what was my mother-in-law's rod-closet, and kneel, asking pardon, which she did with tears. I made her prepare, and I whipped her well. The girl's flesh is plump and firm, and she is a cleanly person—such a one, not excepting my own daughters, who are thin, and one of them, Charlotte, rather sallow, as I have not whipped for a long time. She hath never been whipped before, she says, since she was a child (what can her mother and her late lady have been about, I wonder), and she cried out a great deal."*

In 1657, a London clergyman, the Reverend Zachery Crofton, curate of Saint Botolph's in Aldgate, was prosecuted and imprisoned for whipping his servant-girl, Mary Cadman. The girl was addicted to staying in bed instead of getting on with her work, and to stealing the parson's sugar.

Apparently on the grounds that a man's wife is a piece of property, it was customary in ancient days to beat a wife like a slave. In the Koran, Mohammed justifies the beating of disobedient wives—"remove them into separate apartments and chastise them". Even so comparatively recently as the middle

* Quoted by Wm M. Cooper, *A History of the Rod*, 1868.

63

of the last century, Mr Justice Buller held that a husband was legally entitled to inflict corporal punishment on his wife, provided he did not use a stick of greater thickness than "a man's thumb". In latter-day female emancipation this old ruling, which was mentioned by a London magistrate in connexion with a certain case in 1937, no longer holds good. The husband, aged eighty, accused of beating his thirty-six-year-old wife with a walking-stick, was "found guilty of persistent cruelty".*

In all parts of the world and all through the ages, wherever and whenever slavery has existed, the whip has been the favourite method of securing from these forced labourers the utmost possible amount of work. The chained slaves in the Spanish galleys were whipped whenever they ceased their labours at the oars; at the time when slave labour was employed on the cocoa and coffee plantations in various tropical countries the whip was used to draw from the negro workers the last ounce of effort of which their diseased and dying bodies were capable.

It is questionable, however, if any form of flogging was more universally and more cruelly employed in comparatively modern times than among the negro slaves working on the cotton plantations in the Southern States of America before the Civil War abolished slavery. It represents, this story of persecution and exploitation of human beings, a particularly unsavoury chapter in the history of so-called civilisation. The negroes were the property of the planters. They were bought and sold in the market just like so many cattle, and they were treated like cattle. The law gave the owners of slaves the right to punish and to maltreat their human property so long as they stopped short of actual mayhem or of causing death. Indeed, legislation, such as it was, seems to have been intended more to protect the owners of slaves than the slaves themselves. Thus, according to the Civil Code of the State of Louisiana, "the slave is entirely subject to the will of his master, who may correct and chastise him, though not with unusual rigour, nor so as to maim or mutilate him, or to expose him to the danger of loss of life, or

* *News of the World*, September 5, 1937.

to cause his death". It will be noted that the slave-owner was allowed considerable freedom in his choice of punishment, and an infinite variety of actual forms of torture were available. An Act of Legislature of 1740, which again gave the owner much latitude in his choice of a mode of punishment, and every opportunity to punish severely, read:

"In case any person shall wilfully cut out the tongue, put out an eye, or cruelly scald, burn, or deprive any slave of any limb or member, or shall inflict any cruel punishment other than by whipping, or beating with a horse-whip, cowskin, switch, or small-stick, or by putting irons on, or confining or imprisoning such slave, every such person shall for every such offence, forfeit the sum of one hundred pounds current money."

It is a dreadful commentary upon the inhumanity and the cruelty of man that not only were such laws passed, but that the slave-owners took advantage of them to the hilt. They whipped, beat, tortured, and manhandled the blacks in every way that ingenuity could devise, and for the most trivial of offences.

Mr Fearon, a writer who did much to draw attention to the manner in which the negroes were treated, gives the following first-hand account:

"A few minutes before dinner, my attention was excited by the piteous cries of a human voice, accompanied with the loud cracking of a whip. Following the sound, I found that it issued from a log-barn, the door of which was fastened. Peeping through the logs, I perceived the bar-keeper, together with a stout man, more than six feet high, who was Colonel ——, and a negro boy about fourteen years of age stripped naked, receiving the lashes of these monsters, who relieved each other in the use of a horsewhip; the poor boy fell down upon his knees several times, begging and praying that they would not kill him, and that he would do anything they liked; this produced no cessation in their exercise. At length Mr Lawes arrived, told the valiant Colonel and his humane employer, the bar-keeper, to desist, and that the boy's refusal to cut wood was

65

in obedience to his (Mr L's) directions. Colonel —— said that he did not know what the nigger had done, but that the bar-keeper requested his assistance to whip Caesar; of course he lent him a hand, being no more than he should expect Mr Lawes to do for him, under similar circumstances."*

If the slave had not performed sufficient work during the day to please his master, he was secured to a whipping-post and flogged. Where it was desired to inflict more severe punishment, the victim was stretched face downward on the floor with hands and legs secured to iron rings or to stakes driven into the ground. Another method was to hoist the victim to the ceiling by means of ropes and pulleys.

The slightest form of disobedience or insubordination was often sufficient to earn a beating; and in their lust for punishing their helpless victims, to their eternal shame, the women were every whit as bad as the men.

Occasionally the floggers went too far, and the authorities, reluctant though they might be, were compelled to interfere. The whipping to death of a slave was something the law could not altogether overlook, though in many cases, after a trial which was little better than a farce, the culprit was acquitted. For instance, one Colonel James Castleman, at Washington in 1851, was allowed to go free although he had whipped a slave to death for theft. Not so lucky was another slave-owner named Simon Souther, who, at the Hanover Court, in 1850, was sentenced to five years penal servitude for whipping and otherwise torturing a slave until he died under the punishment. The negro's ordeal before death mercifully intervened was a terrible one. He was bound firmly to a tree, and whipped and better whipped with switches. Souther handled the whip himself until he had to desist from sheer fatigue. He then ordered another negro in his service to "cob Sam with a shingle". Not content with this, he also enlisted the services of a negro woman; and after the three of them had whipped and cobbed the prisoner to their heart's content, they lit a fire and inflicted

* *The Percy Anecdotes*, 1820-3.

burns on his body. Even this did not exhaust the list of tortures that Souther, in his fiendish itch to punish, inflicted upon the helpless slave. He ordered his victim to be washed with hot water containing red pepper; he very nearly strangled him with ropes; he kicked and stamped upon him with his heavy boots until the last flickers of life left the carcase.

A clergyman who saw much of the slave-life of that time, in a book entitled *The Iron Furnace*, gives several instances of flagellations which ended fatally. Thus:

"Mr P——, who resided near Holly Springs (Mississippi) had a negro woman whipped to death while I was at his home during a Session of Presbytery. Mr C——, of Waterford, Mississippi, had a woman whipped to death by his overseer. But such cruel scourgings are of daily occurrence. Mrs F—— recently whipped a boy to death within half a mile of my residence."*

The universality of whipping and its severity were indicated by the statements of the surgeons who examined negroes wishing to enlist in the Federal Armies during the American Civil War. One negro in five, said Mr de Pass, one of the examining surgeons, showed scars resulting from whippings, and in some cases they were of a terrible character, indicating the severity of the floggings, one man showing the marks of over a thousand lashes. Mr Wesley Richards, another surgeon, stated that of those he examined fully half of them presented evidence of flogging or injuries resulting from other forms of punishment.

Nor was this inhuman treatment restricted to the male sex. However chivalrous and lenient the white man may have been to females of his own race, where slaves were concerned the matter assumed quite another aspect. Mr J. M. Ludlow, writing in *Good Words*, quotes the statement of a Mr Nordhoft, who said of a woman slave "she had suffered treatment so inhuman that I cannot describe it here; I will only say that not only her back but her breasts bore deep scars, the marks of

* Quoted by J. M. Ludlow in an article on "American Slavery" in *Good Words*, 1863.

unmerciful and brutal flogging". The same writer goes on to say:

"Solomon Bradley describes the following as the most cruel punishment he ever saw inflicted, by one Mr Ferraby, owner of one of the largest South Carolina coast plantations, near Port Royal. Attracted by the noise of fearful screams in Mr Ferraby's own yard, he went up, and saw a slave-girl stretched on the ground on her face, her hands and feet tied fast to stakes, her master standing over her, beating her with a leather trace from a harness, every blow of which raised the flesh if it did not gash it, and now and then kicking her in the face with his heavy boots when she screamed too loud. When he had become exhausted by this benevolent exertion, our 'patriarch' sent for sealing-wax and a lighted lamp, and dropped the blazing wax into the gashes; after which, finally, his arm being rested apparently, he switched the wax out again with his riding whip. Two grown-up Miss Ferrabys were all this while watching the humane series of operations from the upper windows. And the offence of the girl was burning the waffles for her master's breakfast."*

Where any spark of leniency showed itself the motive behind it was not humanity for the sufferer, but the fear that the market value of the slave might be lowered if the signs of punishment were too obvious. For the slave-owner could not have it both ways: he could not both indulge his sadistic pleasures and get the top market price for the maimed or crippled slave.

Human ingenuity gets over most difficulties however. And human ingenuity is not necessarily devoted to just or humane ends. It is just as often directed to cruel, disgraceful, revolting and disgusting purposes. With the slave-owners it was directed to the finding of a method of punishing the negroes without adversely affecting their market value. It was to an enterprising Virginian 'white' that came the big idea whereby it was possible to 'whip' or beat a negro into insensibility without leaving any

* Quoted by J. M. Ludlow in an article on "American Slavery" in *Good Words*, 1863, p. 829.

traces of the owner's handiwork. To this end, he devised a thin wooden 'paddle' punctured all over its flat surface with small holes. With this instrument, so it was said, a slave could be given such terrible punishment that he lost consciousness, and yet no lacerations, fissures, or other signs of punishment having been inflicted, would result. Another favourite method was the use of a very broad soft leather strap.

One of the major reforms that can be placed to the credit of the rise of civilisation is the abolition of human slavery in its more pronounced and more blatant forms, in all except isolated spots on the earth's surface.

Although the abolition of *human* slavery is well in sight, slavery (in the sense of and to the extent to which the term is indicative of callous ownership without any recognition of the slave's right to enjoy an existence of his, her or its own), in various other forms, still exists. The slaves of today are mainly animal slaves. Horses, dogs and other animals are whipped, punished and tortured terribly. The sadist is here given an almost unlimited field for the exercise of his lust for cruelty. For the various societies for preventing cruelty to animals and for the abolition of cruel sports, admirable as is their work, are only able to touch the fringe of the cruelty that undoubtedly has for long existed. Only the most flagrant cases can be brought into court with any hope of securing convictions—the law, even in these supposedly humanitarian days, looks upon the infliction of torture on an animal as something decidedly less obnoxious and censorious than petty thievery. And for every case that actually gets into the courts one may safely say there are a thousand of which the world never so much as hears.

Cruelty to animals takes many forms apart from and in addition to the slave state, with all its diabolically sadistic connotations, imposed upon such horses, mules, donkeys, dogs and other animals as are pressed into man's service as beasts of burden or in other working roles. Performing animals are still very popular with circus spectators, and it has been proved often enough in the past that such animals are trained by cruel methods.

VII: FLOGGING IN THE ARMY AND NAVY

FROM the time of the Romans flogging was recognised as the most effective form of punishment for soldiers. In those early days it was administered for the most trivial breaches of discipline, and with vindictive and terrible cruelty. Mercy would appear to have been an unknown quality among the officers gracing the military courts-martial. Death was very often the result of these floggings.

For hundreds and hundreds of years in the Christian dispensation, flogging continued to be the main mode of punishment in the armies of Europe. Every guard-house in Germany and in Austria had its whipping-bench, upon which, for the most absurdly small offences, in the blessed name of discipline, the men were flogged unmercifully with rattan canes. In Russia, the country which gave to the world the horrible knout, the favourite method of punishment employed in the Army was known as 'running the gauntlet'. The troops were arranged in two rows, facing each other, each soldier holding a whip or switch. Stripped to the waist, his hands tied securely to the muzzle of his musket, the butt of which was held by a soldier in such fashion that the bayonet point faced the stomach of the culprit, he was ready for the revolting ordeal. Each of his arms was then held by a soldier, and in this fashion he was slowly marched between the two files of waiting troops, who beat him with their whips as he passed. He could not hurry, he could not stop or fall; he was just helpless under the rain of blows. Rarely did he survive the ordeal. Whoever devised this particular form of barbaric torture was worthy of a seat on the Spanish Inquisition itself.

In the English Army, for centuries, flogging seems to have been the customary mode of punishment for almost every offence. It was authorised in the Mutiny Act of 1689, and from that time until the early 1800s, when some efforts were made to abolish flogging, and certain inquiries were instituted, it was used frequently and unmercifully.

According to Major-General Charles J. Napier, whose lot it had been to see the 'cat' used in hundreds of cases, "men are frequently convulsed and screaming, during the time they receive from one lash to three hundred lashes, and then they bear the remainder, even to eight hundred, or a thousand lashes, without a groan; they will often lie as if without life, and the drummers appear to be flogging a lump of dead, raw flesh".*

Sir Francis Burdett, foremost among those agitating for the abolition of flogging, mentioned in Parliament the case of a private being given fifty lashes for making a complaint respecting the bread which was being served to his regiment; and another case where a soldier died after the infliction of 250 of the 1,000 lashes to which he was sentenced. There can, indeed, be no question that deaths were common in both the Army and Navy.

The English cat-o'-nine-tails, the weapon employed, was a terrible instrument of flagellation. It was a close rival of the Russian knout. The 'cat' consisted of nine separate thongs of leather or thick whipcord, each two feet in length, and knotted in three places. At each stroke the thongs cut through the skin like so much paper, the knots tearing out lumps of flesh. The sensation of the whipped individual, says Shipp, is "as though the talons of a hawk were tearing the flesh off the bones", and, as stroke follows stroke, and the 'cat' becomes clotted with blood, it "falls like a mass of lead upon the back".†

Those charged with the whipping of their comrades were

* Major-General Charles J. Napier, *Remarks on Military Law and the Punishment of Flogging*, London, 1837, p. 163.

† John Shipp, *Flogging and Its Substitute*, 1831.

instructed in the art of wielding the 'cat', being trained from boyhood until they became experts. According to the statement of "An Old Artillery Drum Boy", writing in the *Morning Advertiser*, September 1, 1832, in the course of this training a tree was used to represent the body of the prisoner, and the flogger was taught to "throw the cats, first to the left, then to the right, and then with a flourish over the head". "I have stood to the tree until I was quite exhausted," says the writer. "I often think, being brought up to exercise such tyranny, that I should not possess the feelings of a human being." At the end of one of these lessons in whipping, the bark of the tree would often be found reduced to a pulp, a fact which conveys some indication of the state of a man's back after half a dozen drummers in turn had used the 'cat'.*

Accidents have always attended the use of the cat-o'-nine-tails, and the effects, both physical and mental, upon the victim are often tragic. Davidson mentions the case of a fifteen-year-old boy with weak lungs, who was whipped thirteen times in a month, resulting in marked development of phthisis; and another case where fits of epilepsy and loss of consciousness were the sequels to severe punitive flagellation.

Sir Samuel Romilly, writing in his Diary under date April 1, 1806, says:

"Attended the Privy Council upon the examination of Mr Stephens, a lieutenant in the navy, under the statute 33. Hen. 8.c.23. He was charged with the murder of three seamen at Bombay, in the year 1801. They had been flogged without any court martial being held on them; and the punishment was inflicted with such horrible severity that they all three died in less than twenty-four hours after it was over. Stephens had been present at the punishment, but he acted only in obedience to the order of his superior officer, Lieutenant Rutherford."†

* John Gardner, *Flogging Suspended for Ever in the Army and Navy*, London, 1832.

† *Memoirs of the Life of Sir Samuel Romilly*, written by himself, Murray, 1840, Vol. II, p. 133.

And again under date February 16th, 1811:

"I happened today, at dinner at the Duke of Gloucester's, to sit next to Lord Hutchinson, and had a good deal of conversation with him on the subject of military punishments. He is a great enemy to those ignominious and cruel punishments which are now continually resorted to. He told me, that while he was at Gibraltar, a soldier, whose only offence was that he had come dirty upon the parade, was flogged with such severity that he died, a few days after, in consequence of the punishment. He mentioned, too, a very recent instance of a man who had been 30 years in the Guards; and, his conduct there having been irreproachable (he not having, even in a single instance, incurred the displeasure of his officers) had been removed into the veteran battalion in the Tower; and who there, because he had been absent a day, had, at the age of sixty, been sentenced to receive 300 lashes, and had the sentence actually inflicted on him."*

In particular, deaths following military floggings were common in India and other tropical countries. A frequent aftermath of severe flogging was fever, which almost always ended fatally. In the reports concerning such deaths, fever or some other malady was invariably given as the cause, and the flogging which had preceded and caused it was never mentioned.

In all cases, indeed, where the prisoner happened to be in anything short of the most robust health, flogging was a most dangerous procedure. This factor, however, seems to have received no consideration at the hands of either judges or executioners, and medical examination before the flogging, where there was any such examination at all, seems to have been a mere farce. Napier says:

"If a man in prison be ill, he may be succoured in time; but if a man be otherwise ill when he is flogged, though the flogging itself may not kill him, the effect produced by it on an

* *Memoirs of the Life of Sir Samuel Romilly*, written by himself, Murray, 1840, Vol. II, p. 362.

incipient disease, may, and this has often happened. I knew of two soldiers who were flogged at Corfu by the sentence of a general court martial, in 1819: both died, and neither had been punished with unusual severity."*

And further, says the same authority on the subject of military flogging:

"It is impossible to say whether a man can bear his punishment or not; the most experienced surgeon can only guess. . . . The result is, in the best view of the subject, that when a man is tied up to be flogged, his life depends upon a guess, and that guess perhaps made by a young and an inexperienced medical officer."†

John Shipp, a soldier whose duty it had been to inflict many floggings, gives more than one instance where death was due directly or indirectly to the use of the 'cat'. Thus:

"One morning, I attended parade, when a wretched-looking, half-dead young lad was tied up for flogging; but the doctor reported him unfit to receive his punishment, as the wounds on his back, received in a former flagellation, were not healed. He was taken down and sent to the hospital, and in one week after I followed him to his grave. Whether the poor fellow's death was to be attributed to the punishment he had suffered, or to the effect of that punishment on his mind, and consequently on his frame, I cannot take upon myself to pronounce; but I fear that it must be assigned to one or other of these causes."‡

The floggings of mutineers ordered by that brutal monster, Governor Joseph Wall, caused the deaths of three men: Sergeant Armstrong and George Paterson, whose sentences were

* Major-General Charles J. Napier, *Remarks on Military Law and the Punishment of Flogging*, p. 151.

† *Ibid.*, p. 153.

‡ John Shipp, *Flogging and Its Substitute*, p. 13.

74

each 800 strokes; and Corporal Thomas Upton, 350 strokes.*
All died a few days later.†

In many cases the miserable victim, tortured with the fear
of possible repetitions of the punishment, committed suicide.
Shipp gives a case within his own experience.

"When the offender was tied, or rather hung up by the
hands, his back, from intense cold and the effects of previous
floggings, exhibited a complete blue and black appearance.
On the first lash the blood spurted out some yards, and, after
he had received 50, his back from the neck to the waist, was
one continued stream of blood. . . . When the poor fellow was
taken down, he staggered and fell to the ground. His legs and
arms, owing to the intense cold and the long period they had
remained in one position, still continued distended, and he
was obliged to be conveyed to the hospital in a dooly, a kind of
palanquin in which sick soldiers are carried. This unfortunate
creature shortly afterwards shot himself in his barrack-room,
in a sad state of intoxication, and was borne to his solitary pit,
and hurled in like a dog."‡

An example of the terrible disproportion between the extent
of the punishments and the nature of the offences for which
they were inflicted, is given by Tytler, a Scottish advocate and
an authority on military law, who states:

"In 1792 Sergeant George Samuel Grant was sentenced a
thousand lashes for the crime of having been instrumental in
enlisting for the services of the East India Company, two
drummers, knowing them at the same time to belong to the foot
guards."§

* Horace Bleackley, *Some Distinguished Victims of the Scaffold*,
Kegan Paul, 1905.

† For a detailed and horrifying account of the flogging of another
convict named Green, at the instigation of this same Governor Wall,
see page 79.

‡ John Shipp, *Flogging and Its Substitute*, p. 11.

§ Quoted by Major-General Charles J. Napier, *Ibid.*, p. 160.

Possibly no better description of an Army whipping exists than that given by Private Alexander Somerville in his book, *The Autobiography of a Working Man*, of his own experience when serving as a private in the Scots Guards. On May 29, 1832, for the crime of "unsoldier-like conduct on the morning of the 28th instant, in dismounting without leave, when taking his lessons in a riding school, and absolutely refusing to remount his horse when ordered to do so," he was sentenced to 200 lashes with the 'cat'. According to Somerville's description of the 'cat', each of the nine tails was two or three times as thick as ordinary whipcord, knotted in six different places, the lot attached to a wooden or whalebone handle two feet in length. The prisoner was ordered to strip to the waist, and was then tied securely by the ankles and wrists to a ladder. In this position, with his breast pressed against the rungs of the ladder, and his naked back exposed to the executioner, he was ready for punishment. The regimental sergeant-major then commanded Farrier Simpson, the executioner, to do his duty, and the punishment commenced. "I felt," says Somerville, "an astounding sensation between the shoulders under my neck, which went to my toe-nails in one direction, my finger-nails in another, and stung me to the heart as if a knife had gone through my body." This, the first stroke, was followed slowly and methodically by blow after blow, "the time between each stroke seemed so long as to be agonizing, and yet the next came too soon". With the fall of the twenty-fifth blow, the sergeant-major cried "Halt!" This was the signal for Farrier Simpson to give place to another executioner, a young trumpeter who had attained considerable proficiency in wielding the 'cat' through assiduous practice upon a bag of sawdust, and who proceeded to cut into Somerville's ribs on both sides of the body with stroke after stroke, until, with the feeling that his internal organs were bursting, he bit his tongue very nearly in two to prevent crying out in sheer agony. In his own words:

"What with the blood from my tongue and my lips, which I had also bitten, and the blood from my lungs or some other internal part ruptured by the writhing agony, I was almost choked and became black in the face. It now became Simpson's second turn to give twenty-five. Only fifty had been inflicted, and the time since they began was like a long period of life; I felt as if I had lived all the time of my real life in pain and torture, and that the time when existence had pleasure in it was a dream, long, long gone by."

The torture went on, up and down the victim's back, stroke following stroke with excruciating severity and slowness, sometimes a fresh patch of skin being opened, sometimes the first cuts and weals being re-broken or re-entered; until, with the completing of the first hundred, the commanding officer said: "Stop, take him down; he is a young soldier." Bruised and bleeding, with a wet towel covering his back, Somerville was taken to the hospital.

Later, Somerville again entered hospital, suffering from an illness which was beyond any doubt a result of the severe punishment he had received. His own comments upon this illness are of interest:

"I did not then believe that my illness, an eruption of very extraordinary biles, on my back, beneath the place punished, arose from the punishment; and Mr Stewart, I doubt not, gave his opinion conscientiously. But, since the year 1832, I have had opportunities of studying the question, particularly in Spain, and I am now certain that, in almost every case of corporal punishment, there are secondary symptoms; that the violence to the muscular or nervous systems, or to both, or to some quality of the body, which is a mystery to an unprofessional person like me, and probably so to the profession, causes a diseased state of the fluids of the body, which disease takes an inward direction, in some cases settling on the lungs, or other internal organ, enfeebling, and, ultimately, destroying the life of the patient; or it takes an outward direction, as in my case, breaking through the skin in biles, thereby saving the life of the patient; or it remains, festers, inflames, and causes a speedy death by mortification, as in the case of Frederick White, of the 7th Hussars, whom a coroner's jury declared to have died, at Hounslow barracks, from the effects of corporal punishment in 1846."*

According to the statements of Napier, towards the close of the eighteenth century, sentences of from six hundred to a thousand lashes were common; and where the punishment was so rigorous that the whipping had to be stopped before the complete number of lashes had been given, the prisoner was removed to the hospital, and the moment his wounds were healed he was dragged out again to be given the remaining number of lashes. In Sir Charles's own words:

"I, then, often saw the unhappy victim . . . brought out from the hospital *three* and *four* times to receive the remainder of his punishment, too severe to be borne, without danger of death, at one flogging; and, sometimes, I have witnessed this prolonged torture applied for the avowed purpose of adding to its severity. On these occasions it was terrible to see the new tender skin of the scarcely healed back again laid bare to receive the lash. I declare, that accustomed as I was to such scenes, I could not, on these occasions, bear to look at the first blow: the feeling of horror which ran through the ranks was evident, and all soldiers know the frequent faintings that take place among recruits, when they first see a soldier flogged. The bringing a man from hospital to receive a second, and third, infliction, cannot *now* take place."†

We are told that flogging in the Navy was of an even more severe character than was customary in the Army—a statement one is loath to believe.‡ However that may be, the whip was undoubtedly used on the slightest provocation, and often with the most deliberate and inhuman cruelty. In a curious work entitled *Experiences of Flagellation*, there is an interesting

* *The Autobiography of a Working Man*, London, 1848, pp. 298-9.
† Napier, *Remarks on Military Law*, pp. 159-60.
‡ Some dreadful examples were cited in Scott Claver's interesting work, *Under the Lash*, London, 1954.

78

account by an eye-witness of a 'flogging at sea', administered in accordance with the orders of Governor Wall in charge of a convict ship. The victim was a former London shopkeeper named Green, sentenced to fourteen years' transportation. For the alleged crime of aiding in an attempted mutiny, Green, without trial, was sentenced by the Governor to be "flogged with a boatswain's cat until his bones were denuded of flesh". The flogging, which was evidently of terrible severity, did not bring forth a single shriek from the prisoner's lips, and the Governor, in a fit of rage, swore he would "make him cry out, or whip his guts out". In response to entreaties, voiced by more humane onlookers, to cry out and save himself further torture, Green said, "it was now too late, as he felt himself dying and unable to cry out; that he had not avoided it from stubbornness, but concealed his pangs lest his wretched wife, who was down below and knew nothing of his situation, should hear his cries and die with anguish. The flogging was continued until the convulsions of his bowels appeared through his lacerated loins, when he fainted away and was consigned to the surgeon,"* who gave evidence when the Governor, it gives one some slight satisfaction to relate, was subsequently tried and sentenced.

By the Army Act of 1881, flogging was restricted to offenders in military prisons. At the same time administrative action was taken by the Admiralty to curtail flogging in the Navy. Caning of youngsters remained permitted in both the Army and Navy for many years afterwards, however. In the United States Navy corporal punishment was abolished by Act of Congress in 1850.

* *Experiences of Flagellation*, compiled by an Amateur Flagellant, privately printed, London, 1885.

VIII: FLOGGING OF CHILDREN IN THE HOME AND SCHOOL

WITH the widespread popularity of whipping as a form of punishment for transgressors, and as a means of deterring others from committing crime in adult life, it was only to be expected that the whip should rank as an admirable instrument for the correction of children. Solomon's dictum: "He that spareth the rod hateth his son; but he that loves him chastises him betimes"; and his admonition: "Withold not correction from the child; for, if thou beatest him with the rod, he shall not die. Thou shalt beat him with the rod, and shalt deliver his soul from hell", were acted upon to the letter by parents all over the world; and the maxim "Spare the rod and spoil the child" was accepted and considered to constitute full and complete justification for flagellating children of both sexes right through the ages until comparatively recent times—so recent, indeed, that within the memories of those of the present day who have reached middle age must be vivid recollections of the sting of the birch or the cane upon their own person or of its infliction upon friends or relatives.

In the olden days boys and girls both, of working-class parentage, were flogged by their parents at home, and by their employers at work; while the children of the aristocracy received their floggings at the hands of their governesses or private tutors, and later at school. Even so long ago as the days of Ancient Greece, nearly a couple of thousand years ago, if history does not lie the schoolmaster used the birch as an instrument of correction. Homer was flogged by his tutor; so was Horace; and so no doubt were all those who went to school at all.

Indeed, it seems to have ranked as a universal corrective in all countries, the whip, or stick, or analogous fustigating instrument. Even the teachers of religion, and the clergy, seem to have called upon the birch to help ram their arguments home. The monk Udalric, writing in 1087 in the *Coutumes de Cluny*, says: "At prayers, if the children sang badly or fell asleep, the prior or master will strip them to their shirts and flog them with osiers or specially prepared cords." In China, whipping was customary in every school until Confucius put an end to it.

From the days when schools were first established until the beginning of the present century, the birching of boys was inseparable from the discipline of nearly every school in Great Britain. It is mainly because of this system that until quite recently England had a reputation abroad only equalled by that of Germany for school floggings. So general was the practice of corporal punishment that not so very long ago the teacher was popularly and vulgarly referred to as a 'bum bruiser'. Brinsley and Locke expressed themselves strongly in favour of flogging; Udall, the notorious flogger of Eton, had many disciples; as late as 1840 Thomas Arnold was birching with the best of them.

Even princes of royal blood did not escape chastisement. Frederick the Great was flogged repeatedly by his father. Carlyle describes how the young Prince was goaded almost to despair by his suffering at the hands of the old King. In a letter to his mother, he remonstrated thus:

"The King has entirely forgotten that I am his son. This morning I came into his room as usual. At first sight of me he sprang forward, seized me by the collar, and struck me a shower of cruel blows with his rattan. I tried in vain to screen myself. He was in a terrible rage—almost out of himself. It was only weariness, not my superior strength, that made him give up. I am driven to extremity. I have too much honour to endure such treatment, and I am resolved to put an end to it one way or another."

The sons of George III were flogged, at the express wish of that monarch, "like the sons of any private English gentleman, if they deserve it". Madame de Maintenon was whipped by her governess for the smallest of offences, such, for instance, as spilling ink on her dress; Rabelais tells of the scholars at Montagu College being treated like so many dogs; Dr Johnson, who, according to his immortal biographer, was a believer in the virtues of the cane as an incentive to the acquisition of good behaviour and learning, was flogged thoroughly and repeatedly while at school. In fact, he attributed to these floggings his matchless mastery of Latin. "My master whipt me well; without that, sir, I should have done nothing." In this repect he seems to be in agreement with the ancient philosopher, Superanus, who, according to Suidas, was so determined to succeed in his chosen studies that "he never grudged himself either the rod or sharp censure, in order to learn all that the schoolmasters and tutors teach their pupils. He even was more than once seen, in the public baths, to inflict upon himself the most severe corrections." Coleridge, too, speaks in favour of flogging.*

On the other hand, Erasmus was very nearly turned against his studies altogether through the severity of the whippings he received. Milton was flogged at Cambridge, for the practice of whipping was in those days as common at the colleges and universities as in the schools. Voltaire was whipped as a youth; De Pixerécout attributed the gout with which in later years he was afflicted to the continual kneeling on the damp cold flags while being flogged in boyhood; Reveillère-Lepeaux went so far as to attribute the deformity he carried through life to the fustigation he received at school.

Occasionally the floggings were so severe as to cause death. Thus, in *The Percy Anecdotes* there is an account of the trial of a schoolmaster named Robert Carmichael, in 1699, for the

* Samuel Taylor Coleridge, *Specimens of Table Talk.*

82

murder of one of his scholars. According to the evidence, Carmichael gave the boy three successive beatings "and in rage and fury, did drag him from his desk, and beat him with his hand upon the head and back with heavy and severe strokes, and after he was out of his hands he immediately died". An examination of the body revealed stripes on the back and thighs, from which much blood had issued, and livid marks on the head; and the jury found the beating which the boy received to be the cause of death. Carmichael was sentenced to seven stripes and banishment from Scotland for life.

But it was at the famous public schools of Britain that whipping was indulged in so commonly and so savagely as to earn for England the reputation to which I have alluded. Eton, Rugby, Winchester, Shrewsbury, Westminster, Merchant Taylors', and many other halls of learning were famous for their flagellations. The fame of the 'Winton rod', used at Winchester, had even reached the ears of Queen Elizabeth. According to Cooper, the Winchester rod, contrary to the usual custom, was not made of birch but of apple, four selected twigs being attached to a handle of wood. The boy to be punished, says Cooper, "knelt down to the block or bench, and two boys 'took him up'—that is, removed the shirt between the waistband of his trousers and his waistcoat—and then the master inflicted four cuts called a 'scrubbing', or six cuts, called a 'bibling', on which occasion the Bible clerk introduced the victim."*

Flogging appears to have been looked upon by the school authorities as a panacea for every breach of discipline, as the following comments in the *Edinburgh Review* (April, 1830) indicate:

"For all offences, except the most trivial, whether for insubordination in or out of school, for inability to construe a lesson, or to say it by heart, for being discovered out of bounds, for absence from chapel or school—in short, for any breach of the regulations of the school—every boy, below the 6th form,

* Wm M. Cooper, *A History of the Rod*, 1868, p. 433.

83

whatever be his age, is punished by flogging. This operation is performed on the naked back, by the head master himself, who is always a gentleman of great abilities and acquirements, and sometimes of high dignity in the church."

According to Bloch, "Westminster School had an evil reputation from very early times"*. The special rod used at Westminster was notorious throughout English academic circles. Its alleged inventor, Dr Bacher, head-master from 1454 to 1487, was a notorious flagellant. Others of equal notoriety, who were connected at one time or another with the school, were Dr Busby, Dr Parr, and Dr Vincent. In Southey's time the flogging mania reached such a pitch that a school magazine, *The Flagellant*, was issued.

A noted Scottish whipper† was schoolmaster Hacket, of whose activities the following account, culled from the pages of *Chambers's Edinburgh Journal* (November 11, 1843), proves interesting reading:

"The master of the grammar school of a burgh in the central district of Scotland, about seventy years ago, was a worthy Trojan of the name of Hacket, a complete specimen of the thrashing pedagogues of the last age.... Hacket would also, twenty times a day, lay victims across the end of a table, and thrash as long as he could hold with the one hand and lay on with the other. Horsing was one of his highest indulgences or luxuries, and he had an ingenious mode of torture peculiar to himself, by causing the boy to stride between two distant boards while he endeavoured to excite the thinking faculties by bringing a force to bear from behind. Thomas Lord Erskine and his brother Henry were brought up at this school, and remembered Hacket's severity through life, complaining particularly that it was all one whether you were a dull or a bright

* Iwan Bloch, *Sex Life in England*, Panurge Press, New York, 1934, pp. 226-7.

† Even in this second half of the twentieth century, Scotland remains a stronghold of the employment of corporal punishment in schools, the use of the tawse being not uncommon.

boy, for if the former, you were thrashed for your own proper demerits, and if you were bright, you had a monitorial charge assigned to you over the rest, and suffered for all the shortcomings of your inferiors."

Cooper mentions that at Eton, where the whippings were equally notorious, "a charge of half-a-guinea for birch was made in every boy's bill, whether he was flogged or not".* It is probable, however, that there were few cases where the charge was not justified—if one grants the justification at all of charging a parent for the whipping of his son!—for in those days schoolmasters, almost without exception, seem to have worked on the principle that every boy would be the better for a flogging, whether or not he had actually done anything to deserve it.

The author of hymns and religious poems, William Whiting, quiremaster at Winchester College, hit an innocent pupil so hard in the 1870s that the boy ran away that night, and when he was retrieved several days later his weals were still visible.

The practice of whipping was not by any means restricted to boys. Up to one hundred years ago, at the highest-class seminaries, girls were regularly birched. So universal was the practice of punishing breaches of discipline, and peccadilloes of every description, with the infliction of corporal punishment, that governesses were *encouraged* to use the birch, though in some cases parental whippings were inflicted. Lady Anne Barnard, writing of her childhood in the latter half of the eighteenth century, refers to the practice. She tells of the whippings administered to her sisters by their governess. Also her mother inflicted similar chastisements "with her own little white hand, which, though soft, was no slight species of flagellation". Lady Anne, in commenting upon the inadvisability of corporal punishment, says: "Had she (her mother) only endeavoured to prevent our errors instead of correcting them, by the judicious advice which the early knowledge of our

* Wm M. Cooper, *A History of the Rod.*

85

various dispositions might have suggested, how much better would it not have been!"*

That certain female sadists sought positions as governesses in order to indulge in their passion for inflicting pain is certain. Moll affirms there are grounds for assuming that the infliction of corporal punishment in order to secure 'erotic excitement' is much more pronounced in women than in men.†

About the middle of the nineteenth century the birching of girls was the subject of much controversy in several popular family journals, notably *The Queen* and *The Family Herald*; and in 1869 there appeared in the pages of *The Englishwoman's Domestic Magazine* a considerable number of letters from readers on the subject of the flagellation of girls both at school and in the home; and the practice found its strong advocates as well as its denouncers.

In this conflict of opinion, however, there was nothing new. In times when men and women were made of sterner stuff, when blatant cruelty was an everyday occurrence, there were men who were strongly against punishment by whipping. Thus Quintilian:

"With respect to whipping school-boys, though it be an established practice, and Chrysippus is not averse from it, yet, I do not in any degree approve it. First, it is a base and slavish treatment; and certainly if it were not for the youth of those who are made to suffer it, it might be deemed an injury that would call for redress. Besides, if a Disciple is of such a mean disposition that he is not mended by censures, he will, like a bad slave, grow equally insensible to blows. Lastly, if masters acted as they ought, there would be no occasion for chastisement; but the negligence of Teachers is now so great, that, instead of obliging their disciples to do what they ought, they content themselves with punishing them for not having done it. Besides, though you may compel the obedience of a boy, by

* Lord Lindsay, *Lives of the Lindsays; or, a Memoir of the Houses of Crawford and Balcarres*, John Murray, 1849, Vol. II, p. 304.
† Albert Moll, *The Sexual Life of the Child*, p. 319.

using the rod, what will you do with a young man, to whom motives of a quite different nature must be proposed? Not to add that several accidents, which are not fit to be named, may be occasioned either by the fear or the pain attending such punishments. Indeed, if great care is not taken in choosing Teachers of proper dispositions, I am ashamed to say to what degree they will sometimes abuse their power of whipping: but I shall dwell no longer on the subject, concerning which the Public knows already too much."*

Plutarch similarly held that whipping was a suitable punishment for slaves and not for free-born children; that praise and encouragement on the one hand, and blame, reproach and remonstrance on the other, would have good effects, while whipping would harden the hearts of the youthful offenders, and provoke hatred and idleness. Such views were, however, in those long distant days, very decidedly in the minority, and it must be noted that the objections were not concerned with the cruelty of whipping *per se*, seeing that slaves were thought to be fit subjects to endure it, but with its possible effects on certain classes of society.

Most of the ancient philosophers and law-makers were in favour of flogging children, not only as a means of inducing them to conduct themselves well and to tell the truth, but also as an aid to education itself. Plutarch says: "Correct your son in his tender years, nor spare the rod: a branch, when young, may easily be bent at your pleasure." Dr Johnson, in expressing the views we have already noted, merely subscribed to the opinions of more ancient writers and pedagogues, all agreeing to some extent with the views expressed by Superanus, the father of them all, that whipping was a necessary concomitant of education; that the better the flogging the more the learning, presumably on the assumption that whipping was to learning what condiment is to meat.

The reason for the abandonment of birching, which, in

* Quintilian, Book I, iii.

general, occurred about the middle of the nineteenth century,* was mainly due to the growth of Victorian prudery. It was held, and held most strongly, that the exposure of the naked posterior was indecent and immoral, particularly so in the case of girls. The alternative of whipping on the back, or on the loins or the shoulders, was recognised to be much too dangerous a practice. The Puritans were between the devil and the deep sea: in the end, though with some reluctance, there were obliged to abandon the use of the birch altogether. Hand-caning was substituted and held its place for years. But eventually this too practically disappeared.

Now it is undeniable that birching was unnecessarily cruel and degrading. For these reasons, and for these reasons alone, it was high time the practice was done away with. It was to the eternal shame of the governors of such schools as Eton, Harrow, and the like, that birching persisted so long.

Not only was it degrading to the boy who was being whipped; it was degrading to the whipper; and it was degrading to the onlookers. Its tendency was to create in all concerned coarseness and indifference to suffering. In many instances, through repetition, floggings came to be looked upon not as exhibitions of cruelty but as entertainments. The statement of Mr J. Brinsley-Richards, a witness of many school flagellations, is illuminating:

"I felt as I have never felt but once since, and that was when seeing a man hanged. It is true that the eyes and nerves soon get accustomed to cruel sights. I gradually came to witness the executions in the Lower School not only with indifference but with amusement."†

The pendulum has now swung to the other side with a vengeance. In place of the old custom of whipping ummercifully

* Even in 1936, however, it was indicated in a debate in the House of Commons that the birch was still being used, albeit rarely, in some State-aided schools, though it "was customary only in one or two of the bigger public schools, particularly Eton".

† J. Brinsley-Richards, *Seven Years at Eton*, 1883.

and with neither rhyme nor reason, today there is little corporal punishment of any kind in English schools, though it has not been totally prohibited by law in all cases. The well-publicised closing of Court Lees, a 'special school', by the Home Secretary in 1967, and subsequent enquiries into the infliction of corporal punishment and other forms of cruelty in Borstals, came as a shock to a great many people who were unaware that such treatment was still officially condoned.

Most schoolmasters would, in any case, refrain from using the cane unless and until every other means of keeping discipline has been tried and has proved unavailing. But thirty years ago or less, severe canings in schools were commonplace, taken so much for granted that only rarely was attention paid to the subject in the Press. Occasionally, however, a case cropped up where allegations of unnecessary severity were made. Such a case occurred, for example, in 1937, when a complaint was made at a meeting of the Bristol City Council that an eight-year-old boy was caned every day for a whole week. It was alleged that "because he was unable to correctly recite two verses of poetry he received from the head teacher five cuts with a ruler. In a second case, a boy attending another school, as a result of a caning, suffered from split tendons."*

An unsuccessful case, brought the same year at Selkirk Sheriff Court against a head-master, seems to indicate that head teachers are allowed considerable latitude in the infliction of punishment. It was contended by the defending lawyer that "a school teacher was *in loco parentis*. A parent delegated powers to school teachers, and accordingly a school teacher could not be guilty of assault unless it was established that the punishment inflicted was cruel." The accusation was of having punished an eleven-year-old boy "with a leather belt, struck him on the face and beat him on the shoulders, back, and buttocks".†

Instances of the castigation of girls were very much rarer than of boys, but they were by no means unknown. In a letter

* *Bristol Evening Post*, July 27, 1937.
† *The Scotsman*, August 10, 1937.

to the *Dublin Evening Mail* (August 10, 1937), "M.C.", who was the parent of a seventeen-year-old girl pupil at a boarding-school, stated that while on holiday at the seaside, as a result of noticing several marks or bruises on the girl's hips, a doctor was consulted.

"He questioned the girl, and she told us that recently a film book and novel had been smuggled into school by another girl, and that most of the girls got a look at them; they were passed to her one day and she was caught reading them one night. The next morning the mistress sent for her and told her she would be punished if she did not tell where she got them. She refused to do this, and was then brought to her room, where two other teachers assisted in removing her knickers, putting her across the bed, and while they held her there, the mistress gave her twelve strokes of a strap on the hips. The other girl, who later admitted getting the books, received fourteen strokes of birch rods for the terrible crime. . . . I now understand that girls are spanked on the bare hips for the slightest offence against the school rules in this school. The doctor told me that complaints of a similar kind were reported in the *Evening Mail* some time ago, and advised me to report the matter to the Board of Education. It is certain that my daughter will not return to that school. . . ."

PART THREE

RELIGIOUS FLAGELLATION

IX: FLAGELLATION IN MONASTERIES AND NUNNERIES

THE story of flagellation is inextricably mixed up with the story of religion. The heads of every religious order existent in ancient days punished severely any breaking of the rules prescribed by their order, whether by the priests, the monks or the nuns associated with it; and the favourite form which this punishment took was that of whipping. The only difference between the judiciary whipping of the vagrants and criminals of the world, and that administered to religious disciples by their superiors, was that while in the one instance it was something to be eluded if at all possible, in the other it was a punishment to be welcomed as a just discipline. So true was this that, as we shall see later, many officials connected with the religious orders inflicted this punishment upon themselves in the form of self-flagellation, as a penance for real or imaginary sins. Especially was this true of the saints and martyrs, with the doings of which the annals of religion are so plentifully besprinkled.

The early historians are in agreement respecting the custom in many lands of whipping worshippers on certain feast days, and all bear out the fact that these worshippers accepted the punishment resignedly, and that in some cases they even appeared to welcome it—a statement well in accord with the fanaticism on the one hand and the submission on the other hand, which were such marked features of the religious zeal with which followers of all early religious cults were plentifully endowed. Plutarch, referring to the customs of the Lacedaemonians, mentions that at the Feast of Flagellations, held once a year, before the altar of Diana, boys were whipped for hours at a stretch. He says "they suffer it with cheerfulness, and even with joy: nay, they strive with each other for victory; and he who bears up the longest time, and has been able to endure the greatest number of stripes, carries the day". Other writers, notably Mozonius and Cicero, bear out all this, the latter asserting that "I several times heard it said that boys had been whipped to death."

According to Herodotus, at the festival of Isis, held each year at Busiris, thousands of people of both sexes "beat one another", apparently with an industry which well matched their enthusiasm.

There can be little doubt that in all monasteries and nunneries, from the days of their foundation, flagellation was common, so common indeed as to call for little comment in the writings of the earliest of the chroniclers; but, as early as the year 508, there appears to have been a ruling by Saint Cesarius d'Arles definitely prescribing whipping as the form of punishment for nuns failing to observe the regulations of their order. By the eighth century, however, most of the religious orders issued specific rules respecting offences and their punishment.

There was the rule which the Bishop of Usez, Saint Ferreol, made for the prevention and punishment of theft: "let him be chastised with the whip, and with great rigour too. The same punishment ought to be inflicted upon him as upon a fornicator, since it may be justly suspected that his lewdness has induced him to commit theft." Somewhat similar was the rule of the Bishop of Braga, Saint Fructuosus, for dealing with a liar or a thief: "That if, after being warned by the elder monks he neglects to mend his manners, he shall, on the third time, be exhorted in the presence of all the brethren, to leave off his bad practices. If he still neglects to reform, let him be flagellated with the utmost severity." Anything in the way of sexual indulgence was looked upon as an even greater crime than theft and the like, as this same Bishop of Braga's ruling shows:

"If a monk is used to tease boys and young men, or is caught in attempting to give them kisses, or in any other indecent action, and the fact be proved by competent witnesses, let him be publicly whipped." Even to so much as look at a woman was a dangerous practice for a monk in those early days; to speak to one was enough to earn him a mild whipping at any rate; to be alone with one was punished by two hundred lashes or living "on bread and water for two days".

Saint Colombanus, Saint Macarius, Saint Benedict, Saint Benoit, Saint Pacome, Saint Aurelian and others, all drew up rules and regulations respecting the punishments to be inflicted for various offences, in some cases stipulating a prescribed number of lashes for the offence in question, in others leaving the severity of the whipping to the discretion of the abbot or superior in charge of the monastery. In addition to the offences already noted, attempts to escape from the monastery, swearing, gambling, any indecorous behaviour, exhibitions of anger, failure to observe the rules of silence, lewd conversations, immoderate drinking, indulging in noisy conversation or laughter, revealing to outsiders any secrets of the order, and many other peccadilloes, were sufficient to ensure a sound whipping; and any attempts to escape such punishment by the parading of extenuating circumstances or excuses, often merely served to ensure a double dose. In fact here the vindictiveness of the religious leaders showed itself plainly—thus: "If the brothers who have been excommunicated for their faults, persevere so far in their pride as to continue, on the ninth hour of the next day, to refuse to make proper satisfaction to the abbot, let them be confined, even till their death, and lashed with rods." So literally, indeed, were these orders taken, and so rigorously were they carried out, that it was no uncommon thing for a monk to be whipped to death where he stood, or to die later from the injuries sustained during the chastisement.

In fact, the abuses connected with the administration of the 'discipline' caused Cesarius, Bishop of Arles, to remind the abbots and priors that "if the flagellations they inflicted were continued too long upon offenders, so that they died in consequence thereof, they were guilty of homicide".

Although the Bishop of Arles himself, and certain of his brethren, restricted the number of lashes to that prescribed in the laws of Moses, such restriction was by no means general. According to the author of *The History of the Flagellants*, not only was "the punishment of flagellation extended to almost every possible offence Monks could commit", but "the duration of the flagellations was left pretty much to the discretion of the Abbot, either in consequence of the generality of the terms used in the Statutes, or in consequence of some express provision made for that purpose. In the ancient constitutions of the Monastery of Cluny, for instance, which Saint Udalric has collected in one volume, different kinds of offence are mentioned, for the punishment of which it is expressly said, that the offender shall be lashed as long as the Abbot shall think meet."

There were two forms of flagellation in use in the monasteries and nunneries, known respectively as the 'superior discipline' and the 'inferior discipline'. The first named was restricted in its area of application to the upper half of the back and shoulders; the 'inferior discipline' was confined to the buttocks and belly. It is worthy of note that the 'inferior' form was by far the less dangerous, especially if it was restricted to the fleshy parts of the posterior, well removed from the interior and more vulnerable organs.

The flogging itself was often carried out by the abbot or superior personally, though he had the power of entrusting the work to other hands. The universality of the practice and the anticipation that every monk would be whipped for some offence or other, real or imaginary, are indicated by the custom, in many monasteries, of wearing a special shirt which opened at the back to as to facilitate the uncovering of the lower part of the body in preparation for flagellation. In certain cases the monk to be whipped was compelled to divest himself of all his clothing in preparation for flagellation, which was performed in full view of all the inmates of the monastery. Thus, by order of Pope John XII, a monk named Godescal was publicly whipped, among those present being Bishop Otger and Charles the Bald.

In those days women received little respect, and were looked upon as the property of the men to whom they were given in marriage. It is not to be wondered at therefore that in the convents they were considered to be deserving of no more consideration or respect than were the monks in the monasteries. Flagellation was common in the nunneries, and for the most trivial of offences, such as conversing about worldly matters, carelessness in the carrying out of their duties, entering the speaking-room without obtaining permission, and the like.

One of the oldest of the ecclesiastical writers to prescribe the whipping of nuns was Cesarius: "It is just that such as have violated the institutions contained in the rule should receive an adequate discipline; it is fit that in them should be accomplished what the Holy Ghost has in former times prescribed through Solomon." Saint Benedict similarly says: "If a sister that has been several times admonished, will not mend her conduct, let her be excommunicated for a while in proportion; if this kind of correction proves useless, let her be chastened by stripes."

It was the custom in many nunneries for the abbess or superior to undertake the necessary castigation herself, often in a private room, but sometimes in public. In some convents, however, specially selected members of the order were trained in the art of whipping, and in all such cases the punishment was of a more severe character than where an untrained hand administered the discipline. In some cases the sadistic nature of the flogger led to the devising of special whips for adding to the severity of the punishment, in addition to increased skill in the wielding of the scourge. It is said that one such, Jeanne de France, daughter of Louis XI, with fiendish ingenuity, devised a five-spiked silver cross for attaching to the whip, resulting in each stroke inflicting five terrible wounds.

Sometimes the flagellation, as in the case of the monks, was not looked upon as a punishment at all, but as a pleasure, giving rise to hallucinations, sexual ecstasy and masochistic love of God. Thus the Carmelite nun, Maria Magdalena of Pazzi, who lived in Florence towards the close of the sixteenth century, found pleasure in being publicly whipped on her naked buttocks. On one occasion she cried: "Enough! Fan no longer the flame that consumes me: this is not the death I long for; it comes with all too much pleasure and delight."* Another similar case was that of Elizabeth of Genton, who, during the flagellation for which she craved, would cry: "O Love, O eternal Love, O Love, O you creatures! cry out with me: Love, Love!"† In these, and similar instances, much of the pleasure experienced was undoubtedly due to stimulation of the gluteal glands in individuals whose sexual repressions were of such a nature as to induce pathological conditions. The part which flagellation plays in sex will, however, be made clear in a subsequent chapter.

Not always was the whipping of the nuns carried out by their own sex. It was no unusual thing for the priests of the order to handle the thong themselves, and it was in such instances that so very often there entered into it the sexual element to which I have referred.

Nuns used the whip on the buttocks of the monks; and in turn the monks flagellated the nuns. It was indeed a merry and a libidinous game.

The Jesuits in particular were addicted to whipping. Ignatius Loyola, who founded the order, used the whip himself, and, if historical records are anything to go by, he used it to some tune too. Peter Gerson, not content with flagellating those who came to receive the discipline in the ordinary way, according to Cooper, "fell upon the country girls at work in the fields and flagellated them".‡

A peculiar form of flagellation, known as grave-whipping, is

* Quoted by Krafft-Ebing, *Psychopathia Sexualis*, English adaptation of the twelfth German edition, p. 36.
† *Ibid.*, p. 36.
‡ Wm M. Cooper, *A History of the Rod*, 1868, p. 97.

referred to by a correspondent in *Notes and Queries* (March 13, 1852):

"Excommunicated persons were formerly restored to the Church, according to the old *Rituale Romanum*, by the ceremony of whipping their graves. When it was resolved the dead party should be restored to the communion of saints, it was ordered that the body should not be disentombed, but that the 'graves shall be whipped, and while the priest whip the grave, he shall say, "By the authority which I have received I free thee from the bond of excommunication, and restore thee to the communion of the faithful." ' "

X: SELF-FLAGELLATION

ONE of the most remarkable features of the life in the ancient monasteries and convents was the widespread practice of self-flagellation, and many people living today find it difficult to believe that there ever existed persons who would inflict pain upon themselves; just as they greet with scornful unbelief any statement that, either now, or in any other age, there are, or ever were, individuals who will or would willingly allow others to use the whip upon their bodies. In both cases, however, they are wrong. There were in the past both men and women by the thousand who flogged themselves; just as today there are men and women who not only allow themselves to be flogged, but who pay someone to wield the whip.

Now, in the case of religious self-flagellation there were many factors which had a share in promulgating the practice. In the first place it was, in many religious orders, a custom which new recruits seeking atonement were advised to observe; and, for the most part, they would no more have thought of rebelling against the practice than they would have contemplated rebelling against any other of the numerous disciplinary measures they were expected to undertake, or the self-abasing observances to which they promised, in all humility, to submit. Also, those were stern days, when men and women, as I have already observed, were made of harder stuff than they are today, and rebellion against the rules of the order would have led to flogging anyway, and would most certainly have involved far more severe chastisement than anything they would administer to themselves. And although I am not going quite so far as to say, in regard to this self-flagellation, that it was exactly a case of *force majeure*, I do think, in many cases, the hint that most inmates would wish to expiate their sins and transgressions by self-flagellation may have been interpreted as something smelling suspiciously like a command.

There are, however, the strongest grounds for thinking that this explanation by no means suffices in all cases. It certainly does not, for instance, explain the self-flagellation, or the voluntary submission to whipping at other hands, in the so numerous cases of members of the royal houses, and of other exalted personages. It just as certainly does not explain the self-flagellation of the leaders of the various religious bodies, to wit, the saints, the bishops, and so on. For any convincing explanation, in all such instances, we must probe deeper.

In some cases, without doubt, we need look no further than the universal belief in the reputed medicinal and other virtues of flagellation. But here we have to grant the existence of some form of suffering, of some distemper, and a pretty severe attack of it at that—an explanation, therefore, which is obviously restricted considerably in its application, and which in any case would not account, except in relatively few cases, for the continuance of the practice over long periods of time.

Finally, and most importantly, we are compelled to fall back upon the need which so often occurs in the case of religious fanatics—and it must be conceded that all who become monks and nuns *are* inclined to religious fanaticism, if not actually afflicted with religious mania—of finding some means of repressing the worldly cravings which arise irresistibly in their minds; hence the popularity of self-torturing in many and devious ways, of which, in ancient times, flagellation was one of the most widespread. The belief in the efficacy of the voluntary submission to pain or suffering or humiliation, as a means of expiation for a sin or transgression committed against God or the Church, was firmly established; and, indeed, to this day, is an integral part of many varieties of religion. Penance looms largely in the Catholic faith; it ranks as the fourth of the seven sacraments. It was this firm belief which let the leaders of the

99

Churches, in those ancient days, go so far as to whip themselves, or to suffer whipping at the hands of their disciples, to wear sackcloth next to their skin, to martyrise their own flesh, to fast for long periods, to parade about in rags and filth, to humiliate themselves in a hundred different ways. It was, too, this self-same firm belief which caused them, whenever they happened to be beset with temptations, which was a frequent occurrence, to try to dispel such longings by self-punishment and self-humiliation.

One must not overlook the fact that in many cases the priests genuinely believed that self-punishment, being a form of sacrifice, would propitiate the god they worshipped. This provides one of the explanations of all forms of asceticism— from the chastity of Roman Catholic priests to the extreme self-tortures practised by the yogis of Tibet and the fakirs of India. Also, and often coincident with this propitiation of their god, the arousing of the sympathy or compassion of the public, which, inevitably, is connected with any form of martyrdom, was no doubt in the minds of those indulging in self-flagellation.

It was undoubtedly by these and other (true or apocryphal) analogous practices that the saints of old established and retained their reputations. There are for the finding many revealing instances. Thus in *Lives of the Saints Canonized in 1839*, in a reference to Saint Liguori, it is stated that he flagellated himself so severely that "one day his secretary had to burst open the door, and snatch the discipline out of his hands, fearing lest the violence with which he scourged himself might cause his death". And, according to the same authority, Saint Pacificus was accustomed to scourge himself to such an extent "as to fill all those with horror who heard the whistlings of the lash, or saw the abundance of blood which he had shed during the flagellation". Then, too, there was the example set by the Biblical heroes. Saint Paul, revered of all associated with the Christian religion, was staunchly held up as a believer in and a practitioner of self-flagellation. "I keep under my body and bring it into subjection." (1 Cor. ix. 27.) Here, if ever man did,

Nymph whipped by a satyr

From a seventeenth century copperplate by Fialetti

Whipping in the press yard of the Old Bailey

Whipping a negro girl slave

From von Bertall's illustration in *Uncle Tom's Cabin*

A public whipping in Delaware in the early years of this century

he stands self-confessed. And we read in Psalms: "For all day long have I been plagued and chastened every morning."

With all these ideas firmly embedded in the minds of the leaders of the sects, it is a matter for no wonder at all that, in the sincerely professed belief that they were upholding sound apostolic tradition, they prescribed these self-same forms of penance for their followers. Those who failed to mortify themselves, and to practise the discipline necessary to please the Church and to placate their God, would be denied entry into the Kingdom of Heaven. In these modern days of widespread agnosticism and atheism it is difficult, almost to the extent of bordering on the impossible, for the mind to realise just how powerful were these arguments of the Church, backed up, as they so effectually were, by the practices of the priests, the bishops, and the saints themselves. To be denied the benefits of the Church, and the expectation of a future existence in Heaven, would be far worse than a denial of a long life on this earth. It was mainly for these reasons that kings and nobles performed their humiliating and painful penances with all the ardour of their subjects.

The cunning priests, too, preying upon the ignorance, the superstition, and the credulity of the day, were not slow to call to their aid apocryphal accounts of benefits resulting to those who flagellated themselves, and of the ill-effects following upon any failure to do so. In their own way, and allowing for the limitations of the age in which they lived, these early propagandists of religion could bring to their aid species of ballyhoo which were every whit as effective as the modern methods of publicity agents. There were the stories told of the power of severe and regular whipping to change the soul's destination from Hell to Heaven; there was at least one account given currency respecting the self-flagellation indulged in by a gathering of priests around a dead monk's bed causing him to come back to life; there was the tale, whispered into credulous ears, that those who refused to whip themselves, or to be whipped while upon this earthly sphere, were scourged good and plenty by every spirit inhabiting Purgatory.

Sex entered largely into the matter, fornication being one of the major sins against the dictates of the Churches. Self-punishment of various kinds were favourite methods adopted by the early saints to subdue sexual thoughts and cravings. There is a story that Peter the Hermit was compelled to lock himself up in his room and take the whip to his own flesh, in order to prevent himself seducing a pretty girl whom he had rescued from the clutches of a satyr. And although this particular story may be of dubious authenticity, there can be no manner of doubt that such-like self-punishments were very often thought to be necessary to subdue licentious thoughts and libidinous cravings.* It was because of the urgency of these repressive measures that the saints, judging every other individual by their own standards, prescribed similar fustigations, tortures and humiliations in every case and circumstance. It is in just the same way that the modern theologian, moralist, or Puritan, finding certain measures essential for the subduing of his own libido, endeavours to make similar taboos or repressive measures universal in their application.

There are indications that self- or voluntary flagellation existed long before the establishment of monasteries and convents, though in most of the recorded cases there are grounds for surmising that they were of a sexual rather than a religious origin. Thus Herodotus, in referring to the custom among the Egyptians, at certain festivals, after feasting, and the offering of sacrifices to their god, of men and women, to the tune of some thousands, whipping each other to their hearts' content, said he was "not allowed to mention the reason why these beatings were performed". Apuleius speaks of priests who whipped themselves with scourges which they carried about with them for that express purpose.

Although the rules of the early monastic orders preserve a

* The complete inability of the ancients to recognise that this so-called "mortification of the flesh" was likely to have precisely the opposite effects to those intended is well brought out by Dr Walter Braun in his excellent book, *The Cruel and the Meek* (Luxor Press, 9s. 6d.; pp. 147 and 166).

discreet silence respecting any self-flagellating practices, this, says the author of *The History of the Flagellants*,

"has been amply compensated in subsequent rules. Thus, the Carmes are to discipline themselves twice a week; the Monks of Monte Cassino, once a week; the Ursuline Nuns, every Friday; the Carmelite Nuns, on Wednesdays and Fridays; the Nuns of the Visitation, when they please; the English Benedictines, a greater or less number of times in the week, according to the season of the year; the Celestines, on the eve of every great festival; the Capuchin Friars, every day in the week, etc."*

But if in the rules of the orders this reticence was observable, biographers and historians were governed by no such scruples.

Chroniclers of the lives of the early Christian theologians refer to various devotees of the cult of self-flagellation. There was Saint Pardulph, who removed every atom of clothes during Lent, and was thrashed daily, in accordance with his own orders, by a disciple. Others wielded the whip themselves. There was Saint William; there was an abbot of Pontoise, by name Gualbertus; there was Abbot Guy of Pomposa; there was Saint Romnald; and there were various personages of lesser importance. The usual practice was to flagellate daily, continuing the process as long as it took to sing or to recite selected psalms or other Biblical passages.

All this flagellation among the saints and the monks, however, appears to have been sporadic up to, at any rate, the end of the first thousand years of the Christian era. Propaganda for flagellation, such as it was, remained restricted more or less to the somewhat crude accounts of benefits received by flagellants, conveyed by word of mouth from one worshipper to another. It was not until the year 1056 that a certain newly created Cardinal, by name Peter Damian de Honestis, initiated a campaign to popularise flagellation. The result of this campaign was to set the whole of Christendom using the whip. Kings and commoners, theologians and criminals, nobles and

---

* *The History of the Flagellants*, 1777, p. 113.

peasants, vied with each other in the avidity with which they whipped themselves and one another.

It is mainly to the writings of this same Damian that we are indebted for much of the information available respecting the practice of self-flagellation among the theological leaders of his time. As an instance, Saint Dominic Loricatus was accustomed to divest himself of every stitch of clothing, and, wielding a birch in each hand, flog every part of his body within his reach, continuing the fustigation as long as it took him to recite the psalter—not once—but three separate times from beginning to end. On special occasions, it appears this same saint whipped himself while singing through the entire psalter "twelve times over", a procedure which filled even the grim, sadistic and fanatical Cardinal "with terror when he heard of it". Another notable self-flagellating monk was Saint Rodolph, who shut himself up in his cell, and sang through the whole psalter to the accompaniment of vigorous whipping.

Now, all modern scepticism notwithstanding, and allowing for the exaggeration which is one of the major sins with which propagandists are so often afflicted, it may be set down as a solid fact that many of these accounts of the self-flagellatory practices of the saints and their disciples are perfectly true accounts. Anyone who has dug deeply into religious origins and practices, pagan and civilised, and who is thoroughly acquainted with the genesis of the various faiths which at one time or another have swept the world, is well aware of the lengths to which, in their fanaticism, men and women will go. And these accounts of the self-flagellation of the ancients, in a considerable number of instances, are supported by evidence of a nature sufficient to establish, beyond any reasonable doubt, the existence of the phenomenon. At the same time, one must not close one's eyes to the fact that many of the stories which have been made much of by credulous writers, have gathered, in travelling down the ages, a good deal of fictitious trimming; and that, apart from the carefully suppressed motives which no doubt prompted many religious leaders to stage their exhibitions, there were undoubtedly many instances in which hallucinations entered into the matter. It is highly probable that, in numerous cases, vivid imaginations transformed a soft whip into a terrible knout; a few slight weals on the buttocks into a blood-striped body.

The use of other and more agreeable disciplinary methods is mentioned by the author of *The History of the Flagellants* in a notable passage which reads:

"Indeed, an infinite variety of instruments have been used for that purpose, whether they were contrived at leisure by the ingenious persons who were to use them, or were suddenly found out, from the spur of some urgent occasion. Thus, incensed Pedants, who could not quickly enough find their usual instrument of discipline, have frequently used their hat, their towel, or, in general, the first things that fell under their hands. A certain gentleman, as I have been credibly informed, once flagellated a saucy young fish-woman with all the flounders in her basket. Among saints, some, like Dominic the Cuirassed, have used besoms; others, like St Dominic, the founder of the Dominican Order, have used iron chains; others, have employed knotted leather thongs; others have used nettles, and others, thistles. A certain saint, as I have read in the *Golden Legend*, had no discipline of his own, but constantly took, to discipline himself with, the very first thing that came under his hand, such as the tongs for the fire, or the like. St Bridget, as I have read in the same book, disciplined herself with a bunch of keys; a certain lady, as hath been mentioned in a former place, used a bunch of feathers for the same purpose; and lastly, Sancho did things with much more simplicity, and flagellated himself with the palms of his hands."

It is highly probable, too, that many flagellations of which sanguinary accounts were given, never actually took place at all. We see indications of this in the numerous stories of the saints being flogged by the devil—stories which are either due to hallucinations, or are plain fabrications. Saint Anthony describes one such incident. Saint Hilarion was repeatedly belaboured by Satan, who, says Saint Jerome, "bestrides him, beating his sides with his heels, and his head with a scourge". And there is the remarkable account given by the famous Saint Francis of Assisi concerning his struggle with and terrible flagellation at the hands of the devil, which rendered essential his hurried departure from Rome, a tale which is bound to arouse suspicion in any logical mind when it is coupled with the fact that the inhabitants of that city gave the saint plainly to understand that he was not wanted, and that his stay might involve danger to himself.

The necessity for absolution caused many a royal personage to submit to the discipline of the whip, and there can be small enough doubt that the knowledge that flagellation, voluntary or otherwise, would atone for sins of pretty nearly every description had a good deal to do with the popularity of the practice among the rich and the powerful. I have an idea that there are today men by the hundred who would gleefully submit to the pain and humiliation of birching if this represented the utmost penalty they would be called upon to pay as punishment for the commission of a major crime.

In English history, we have the well authenticated case of King Henry II. His resentment against Thomas à Becket, his Archbishop of Canterbury, had led him, in a fit of passion, to say "what sluggard wretches, what cowards, have I brought up in my court, who care nothing for their allegiance to their master: not one will deliver me from this low-born priest". It was a most unfortunate speech, even for the King, in view of the subsequent assassination of the Archbishop, and there were those who were not slow to accuse Henry of complicity in the murder. As an act of atonement he allowed himself to be flogged in Canterbury Cathedral. Nor was this any isolated example. Prince Raymond VI was whipped in Valencia, at the Church of Saint Giles; the Emperor Henry submitted regularly to flagellation; Foulques, Count of Anjou; William, Duke of Aquitaine; Raymond, Count of Toulouse, all allowed themselves to be whipped. And, in the eleventh century, one of Italy's leading aristocrats, the Marquis of Tuscany, was flogged by an abbot in the church.

Henry IV of France was more wily. When, after excommunication, he was ordered to submit to flagellation for the securance of absolution, he instituted the system of vicarious punishment, whereby the guilty and atoning party could hire someone to take his place. Two of his ambassadors, by name Du Perron and D'Ossat, at his request, submitted their bodies to the strokes of the rod in his stead. Shortly afterwards they blossomed into cardinals, which fact seems to indicate the nature of the reward promised them for their services. This was in 1595, and the practice thereafter seems to have been expanded even to the lengths of self-flagellation, men being willing to flog themselves as a measure of atonement for the sins of anyone prepared to pay their fees.

The fair sex, too, adopted flagellation as a means of securing absolution. Maria Magdalena, a Carmelite nun, flogged herself nearly every day, as well as submitting to flagellation by others (cf. Chapter IX). So, too, did Catherina of Cordona, another nun belonging to the Carmelite order: she ended her career as a raving lunatic. Saint Hardwigge, Saint Hildegarde and Saint Maria, are all examples of women who attained notoriety through self-flagellation. Queen Anne of Austria allowed the discipline* to be administered to her by one of the Benedictine confessors.

But, if we are to accept the testimony of Damian, the earliest authority on flagellation, there was one woman, known as the widow Cechald, who easily capped the lot. A lady of gentle birth and of no little dignity, she lashed herself no fewer than three hundred times. It certainly seems a tall story, and we may be excused for doubting the reverend historian's accuracy, or, alternatively, marvelling at his credulity.

Church Councils frequently ordered penitents to submit to the discipline. They had no recourse but to obey, and the punishments they submitted their bodies to, cheerfully or

* Originally, flagellation as a form of religious penance, was known as *disciplina flagelli*, but eventually, as a result of its widespread employment throughout Europe for this purpose, the term *discipline* came to be a synonym for flagellation and for flagellation alone.

otherwise, were terrible, and, to modern ears, incredible. Apropos of this, Lea says:

"Stripped as much as decency and the inclemency of the weather would permit, the penitent presented himself every Sunday, between the Epistle and the Gospel, with a rod in his hand, to the priest engaged in celebrating mass, who soundly scourged him in the presence of the congregation, as a fitting interlude in the mysteries of divine service. On the first Sunday in every month, after mass, he was to visit, similarly equipped, every home in which he had seen heretics, and receive the same infliction; and on the occasion of every solemn procession, he was to accompany it in the same guise, to be beaten at every station and at the end. Even when the town happened to be placed under interdict, or himself to be excommunicated, there was to be no cessation of the penance, and apparently it lasted as long as the wretched life of the penitent, or at least until it pleased the inquisitor to remember him and liberate him."*

* Henry Charles Lea, *A History of the Inquisition of the Middle Ages*, Macmillan, New York, 1906, pp. 464-5.

XI: THE SECT OF THE FLAGELLANTS

EVERY student of sociology is well aware of the inherent gregariousness of man. It goes far beyond the gregariousness of animals or birds, which is purely physical. In mankind it is physical, spiritual and mental. It is just as dominant a force, this gregariousness, in man's make-up today as it was in the earliest stages of civilisation, and in the Middle Ages. This gregariousness, which was at the root of those manifestations which, in past ages, have shown themselves as various communal manias, such as mass dancing, demonology, witchcraft, religious crusades, and in many other ways, is similarly at the root of many present-day mass phenomena such, for instance, as national advertising campaigns, the radio, television, the cinema, the popular Press.

The response of masses of men and women to suggestion has always been the basis of every religious, political or social movement. The actions or responses of an individual member of society to given stimuli can never be foreshadowed with any degree of certainty; the actions or responses of mankind in the mass can be predicted with mathematical exactitude. It is to this more than to any other fact that charlatans, quacks, political mountebanks, dictators, revivalists, and other merchants of mush, owe their success.

Now, of all movements which owed their inspiration to waves of emotion, none has ever transcended in spectacularness, fanaticism and (to observers in other ages) incredulity, the successive waves of voluntary flagellation which punctuated the annals of the thirteenth, fourteenth, fifteenth and sixteenth centuries.

There seems to be some doubt as to where precisely the first public flagellating movement broke out, or who exactly was the individual responsible for the actual genesis of the idea; but certainly Saint Anthony seems to have had a good deal to do with it. Unless the chroniclers of the age lie, he went about the country preaching to sinners about the wrath of God, on the need for repentance and atonement, much in the manner of a modern drum-banging revivalist; and, in the early twelve hundreds, he appears to have set in motion the first serious organised procession of men and women beating each other with the express object of establishing themselves in the good books of their God and earning a pass to Heaven.

Around the year 1260, fresh impetus was given to the movement through the efforts of an Italian hermit and fanatic by name Ramier, a Dominican. Italy at the time was passing under a black cloud. Her list of misfortunes, through one cause and another, was apparently endless. Ramier, in the true religious spirit of the age, argued that penance was the only way to avert disaster, and, at that, penance of such a widespread nature as would surely suffice to atone for all that was inducing the anger of Jehovah.

Men, women and children in their birthday suits, and carrying nothing but thongs of hide, walked in solemn procession, praying to God for forgiveness, weeping, groaning, and, every few moments, lashing the persons nearest them with the scourges they carried. These processions of penitents were everywhere. The priests, carrying banners and wearing crosses, made up the van of the procession. To the tune of ten thousand eager souls, they marched, these fanatics, through Italy; they crossed the Alps; they 'invaded' Bavaria, Alsace, Bohemia, Poland, and at every step and in each country, they gathered recruits, swelling their ranks enormously and rapidly. "Those who were at enmity with one another became friends. Usurers and robbers hastened to restore their ill-gotten riches to the rightful owners. Criminals confessed. The doors of the gaols were opened and the prisoners released, those who had been banished from the country were allowed to return. In short, Christian charity, humility and good will prevailed."

But despite its remarkable popularity with the masses, the movement met with a good deal of opposition from the leaders of other and rival faiths. It met with a good deal of ridicule too. All this is not to be wondered at, being the common lot of most new religious cults. It has been the lot of the Mormons, of the Perfectionists, of the Spiritualists, of the Theosophists, of the Christian Scientists, of the Dukhobors, of the Shakers, *et al.* Two thousand years ago, it was the lot of Christianity itself.

In 1349 the movement swept through Germany like a whirl-wind, however. At that particular time the country was being ravaged by a plague known as the Black Death. The German movement was apparently initiated in the town of Spira, where the Flagellants went through their ritual in full view of the onlookers who gathered to watch them. Divesting themselves of all their clothes except their shirts, they lay on the ground in various postures, and were whipped, either by the priest in charge or by one another, to the accompaniment of psalm-singing, prayers to God against the plague, and other appeals. When the flagellating performance was concluded, says Albert of Strasbourg, a contemporary historian:

"One of the brotherhood rose, and with a loud voice read a letter, which he pretended had been brought by an angel to St Peter's Church, in Jerusalem; the angel declared in it that Jesus Christ was offended at the wickedness of the age, several instances of which were mentioned, such as the violation of the Lord's Day, blasphemy, usury, adultery, and neglect with respect to fasting on Fridays. To this the man who read the letter added, that Jesus Christ's forgiveness having been implored by the Holy Virgin and the angels, he had made answer that in order to obtain mercy, sinners ought to live exiled from their country for thirty-four days, disciplining themselves during that time."

From Spira they moved to Strasbourg, recruits joining, solidly and enthusiastically, on the way, so that by the time the procession left this latter town, it numbered all of a thousand strong.

After this, however, the sect met with constantly increasing opposition from influential quarters. The Pope opposed the movement; the Inquisition tortured and executed its leaders. And so, for a time, the Flagellants were compelled to pursue their cult in secret and as best they could, until, towards the close of the sixteenth century, the movement again burst into activity. In France, in particular, the cult spread throughout the whole country, infecting Paris itself and attracting the attention of many influential personages. Then, with the conversion, first of the Queen-Mother to their tenets, and later of King Henry III himself, the supremacy of the Flagellants was complete and their standing assured for the time being. There were soon many different bands or branches operating in various parts of France. The King, in 1585, formed a new band known as the Brotherhood of the Annunciation Day, with the Cardinal of Lorraine, the Duke of Mayenne, the Cardinal of Guise, the leading courtiers and ministers, and other members of the aristocracy, as principal officials. The Cardinal of Lorraine, after one of the public demonstrations, took to his bed and died within a few days, and the tale is told that his fatal illness was due to severe whipping and exposure.

Following the example of their lords and masters, the women took up public flagellation, joining the processions. At first, the more bashful among them, it is true, waited until darkness provided a protective screen for their performances; others, with official approval, wore masks; others again contented themselves with the mere carrying of whips; but as the number of females, and especially of aristocratic ladies, taking part in these processions increased, they shed all decorum and bashfulness, in the end entering into the performance with all the zest and vigour of the men. "After the death of the Guises," says Cooper, "the fanatical mania for fleshly mortification revived, and this time women and maidens, naked to the shift, ran about with whips. Noble ladies showed themselves to the populace in a semi-nude state, and gave themselves the discipline, in order to encourage others by their example."*

* Wm M. Cooper, *A History of the Rod*, 1868, p. 111.

But although the cult was blessed with royal support, as it happened, this did not suffice to render it impregnable. King Henry III of France, his royal blood notwithstanding, was no Czar able to flaunt hostile criticism with impunity, or possessing the power to consign to prison, or to exile, those who failed to genuflect to him in word and deed. There was, at the time, an opposition element of some power, and the members of this opposing party did not fail both to criticise and to heap scorn upon the antics of the King and his associates. Also, as was natural, there was once again a good deal of opposition from the leaders of orthodox religion. One opponent, John Gerson, no less a personage than Chancellor of the University of Paris, published a treatise pointing out the evils of flagellation, which he alleged was a cruel and an evil practice, contending that it should be held by the authorities to be as unlawful as castration or mayhem.

Others hymned the same tune until, in response to the gathering trend of public opinion, in the early sixteen hundreds, Parliament took action, prohibiting public flagellation and proclaiming all members of the sect to be heretics.

This, so far as France was concerned, was the beginning of the end. There were, true enough, for the finding, scattered remnants of the once powerful bands. These practised their cult surreptitiously and behind closed doors, but no public demonstrations or processions flourished or were even attempted. In other parts of Europe there were sporadic efforts to revivify the movement, but they met with little success. Cooper mentions that Father Mabillion claimed to have seen "a scourging procession of the Flagellants at Turin on Good Friday 1689"; that in 1710 there were processions still to be seen in Italy; that Colmenar "mentions a procession taking place in Madrid"; that as late as 1820 Flagellants appeared in public in Lisbon.* Long after this, too, private 'whipping clubs' flourished secretly, but it is highly probable that these were then, as certain somewhat similar 'societies' of today are now, using the cloak of religion to cover purely erotic purposes.

* Wm M. Cooper, *A History of the Rod*, 1868, p. 113.

And so passed into oblivion as strange a manner of stimulating religious ecstasy and fervour as the world has ever seen.

In marvelling, in these supposedly enlightened days, over the survival for centuries of such a remarkable religious phenomenon, one must never overlook the fact that all religions owe much of their success to their spectacularness. The dramatic has always been an essential feature of any religious cult, and the more effective the show presented, the greater the success of the cult. All through the ages we see examples of this in the flourishing of half a hundred different faiths, all presenting the same fundamental quackeries, decked out in half a hundred different gaudy wrappings, and presented on half a hundred different dramatic stages. The Protestant faith always depended much on its ceremonial, its rubric, its empiricism, its ritual; the Roman Catholic faith outdid it, and thus scored a wider and a more lasting success. In the early days of Christianity, there was nothing else in the way of appeals to the dramatic that could, so far as the masses were concerned, move them to admiration and acceptance as did the shows staged by the Churches. Even today, when religion in Europe and America seems to be moribund or even gangrenous, any temporary flare-up that it is able to stage is connected with the putting on of a new and a free show. The showmanship of the Revivalists, of the Aimee MacPhersons, Billy Sundays, Woodbine Willies, Faith Healers, Billy Grahams, and so on, succeed in filling the temples, stadiums and arenas, spasmodically at least, simply because the old, old act is being staged in a new dress.

It will surely be evident that with the rivalry of the cinema, television, and a score of other appeals to the dramatic, the shows that the Churches can stage are, in the main, old-fashioned and crude. Moreover, the increased prosperity of the masses has largely negated the appeal of free entertainment. They prefer to pay to go to the theatre or a night-club rather than accept anything which the Churches have to offer for nothing (except what is put in the collection plate).

The influence of suggestion still exists. It is still powerful.

But it works in different ways; it calls for different modes of presentation. Newspaper and television campaigns, with their strong emotional appeals, today have largely taken the place once held almost exclusively by religion.

Looking back through the centuries, as history depicts them, it is easy for the student of sociology to understand the influence which exhibitions of self-flagellation had upon the masses. Its dramatic element, and its suggestive powers, were considerable. Its reputed painful nature merely served to increase its dramatic effects. And much of the anguish associated with it was apocryphal. The ancient pedlars of religions staged their shows with all the skill of the moderns. There is a deliciously ironical suggestion about the account given by an eye-witness of one of the flagellating services held during Lent in the Church of the Caravita in Rome. The service lasted a quarter of an hour, during which time the church was in total darkness, and judging from the sounds, some worshippers were using whips and others their hands. "Hundreds," says this writer, "were certainly flogging something, but whether their own bare backs, or the pavement of the church, we could not tell."*

* James Gardner, *The Faiths of the World*, p. 901.

XII: THE HOLY INQUISITION AND
FLAGELLATION

IF ever anyone cares to dredge from the records of the past an account of the persecutions, cruelties and tortures, and to fix the guilt upon the parties responsible for these same persecutions, cruelties and tortures, it will be found that religious leaders and fanatics have had the dismal honour of planning and perpetrating the major share of them. The history of religions is the history of man's cruelty to, persecution of, and intolerance of, man. The moment an individual, whether man or woman, becomes fired with an excess of religious zeal, that individual becomes plainly insufferable to any intelligent person. More, the religious crusader, fired with proselytising passion, becomes a potential danger to the liberty of the people. In these days, when the development of science and the machine age have shorn Christianity of much of its power, followers of rival faiths, agnostics and atheists, are enabled to parade their heresy publicly with little in the way of social ostracism, and certainly without any danger to their life and limbs. It was not always so. The tolerant attitude of today is of quite modern growth. Until comparatively recent times expressions of opinion which today arouse no comment or criticism, would have earned for their speaker or writer social ostracism, if not actual imprisonment. I have myself put into print opinions, which, twenty years earlier, would have been enough to endanger my personal liberty, and which a couple of centuries ago would surely have caused me to be burned at the stake.

Glancing back through a catalogue of the terrible deeds which will for ever blacken the cause of Christianity, the enormities perpetrated by those religious dignitaries who formed the council of the 'Holy' Inquisition cause all others to look like mere schoolboy pranks. One can only account for such deeds by the supposition that those appointed to try and to sentence men and women who fell into the clutches of this Inquisition, and those responsible for the actual carrying out of the sentences, were religious sadists beside whom the notorious Marquis de Sade pales into insignificance; or men whom religion had transformed into maniacs or fiends.

There is a grim irony in the fact that ostensibly the Inquisition was created as a *Court of Justice* or a Sacred Tribunal. The idea of the thing seems to have been born in the head of one of the Dominican monks. The first of these courts was at any rate created by the Dominicans, and approved by the Pope. This was in about the third decade of the thirteenth century. Once started, the scheme caught on in all the Roman Catholic countries.

Originally the idea was to form a sort of ecclesiastical court for trial and punishment of various offences against the canons of approved religion. But although witchcraft, astrology, divining, fortune-telling and various allied offences were dealt with by the court, its main efforts were concentrated on the rigorous punishment of heresy.* Indeed, whatever precise reasons may have been given to justify the establishment of the Inquisition, there can be no doubt that the furtherance of the Roman Catholic religion, by putting into all dissenters the fear of God's wrath, was the primary reason for its establishment, its expansion, and its continued existence through the centuries.

* From a careful search of historical records it would appear that the first law to be passed with the express object of suppressing heresy was that of A.D. 382, whereby heretics were condemned to death. The officers empowered to ferret out heretics, and to punish them, were called Inquisitors; but unlike the ecclesiastical officers who, a thousand years later, were appointed by the Pope and his minions, these early Inquisitors were laymen selected for the job by the Church. Although the Inquisition never extended its tentacles into England, heresy even here, under an Act of 1400, was punishable by death.

It is true that the campaign against heresy, real or alleged, had always been waged whenever and wherever opportunity offered. It is further true that drastic punishments, even to the extent of execution,* had been often enough the lot of those caught practising or promoting rival cults. There was, however, no uniformity in the punishments meted out to heretics: in some cases excommunication was deemed sufficient; in others imprisonment; and in yet others death by burning. Trials were in some cases conducted by the Church, but more often by the civil authorities.

The growing power and effrontery of certain influential sects of dissenters led to the Church asking kings and princes to tighten up the regulations respecting the persecution of heresy, and finally to decree that the matter was one best handled by the Church itself. All this undoubtedly had much to do with the foundation of the Inquisition as a permanent court for dealing specifically with this particular crime.

For a matter of centuries the Church of Rome had been having considerable trouble with a rebellious sect known as the Albigenses.† They were rebels, and powerful rebels at that. Actually, their only heresy lay in the fact that they were opposed to some of the doctrines, and refused to accept the autocracy, of the Catholic Church. They were devout

---

* "If there be found among you, within any of thy gates which the Lord thy God giveth thee, man or woman that hath wrought wickedness in the sight of the Lord thy God, in transgressing his covenant,

"And hath gone and served other gods, and worshipped them, either the sun, or moon, or any of the hosts of heaven, which I have not commanded;

"And it be told thee, and thou hast heard of it, and inquired diligently, and, behold, it be true, and the thing certain, that such abomination is wrought in Israel;

"Then shalt thou bring forth that man or that woman, which have committed that wicked thing, unto thy gates, even that man or that woman, and shalt stone them with stones, till they die." (Deuteronomy xvii. 2-5.)

† The term was usually and originally applied to the sect which established itself under the protection of Raymond, Count of Toulouse, in the district of Albigia. In time, however, it became a general term employed by the Roman Church to describe every sect which failed to accept its doctrines.

Christians, worshipping the anthropomorphic Godhead of Christianity. The accounts of their immorality, their blasphemies, their sexual perversions, and various other crimes, were purely fictitious, manufactured by the priests of Rome to justify a monstrous and otherwise inexcusable campaign of persecution.

The Church of Rome marshalled all its resources, it called upon all princes and potentates owing allegiance to the Pope, to unite in a crusade against the Albigenses. It entered upon a war which was to be waged with unrelenting fierceness until the so-called heretics were dispersed or exterminated. The leader of one sect of heretics, Raymond VI of Toulouse, was excommunicated by the Pope, forced to hand over his seven castles to the Church, and, probably to save himself further persecution and possibly his own skin, he submitted his body to the whip. At the Church of Saint Agele, by order of the Pope, the Count was flogged to such an extent that it was impossible for him to restore the clothes to his torn and bruised body.

It was, then, in the midst of this strife, and with a view to putting very thoroughly into all dissenters the fear of torture and death, that the Church of Rome founded 'the Holy Inquisition', and it was at Toulouse that the first of these courts was held. There seems to be some doubt as to which of two individuals was responsible for the idea of this scheme which was destined to become as notorious as it was feared throughout all the marches of Europe, and to go down in history as the most terrible blot upon the annals of religion the world has ever known. Some historians give the credit to Pope Innocent III; others contend that Dominic, founder of the order of friars bearing his name, was responsible for the birth of the notion. Probably, if the truth could be got at, both had a finger in perfecting the scheme, for both were obsessed, to the point of fanaticism, with the idea of punishing heresy. At any rate, this Dominic was placed in office as the first Inquisitor-General.

The first court was followed by the establishment of others in various parts of France, of Spain, of Germany, of Italy, of Portugal. Those found guilty of heresy were variously convicted to slavery in the galleys, to perpetual imprisonment, to be burned at the stake.* The capital sentence, in reality, was a work of mercy, for all who were not burned, were whipped and tortured continuously until death supervened. Men and women were haled into the courts on the slightest of pretexts, and their conviction, once they came before the Inquisitor-General, was sure to follow automatically. False evidence was concocted against them, and they were whipped and tortured until they confessed to whatever crime had been fixed on them. Anyone's evidence against the accused was accepted without question by the court. Indeed, to call the Inquisition chamber a court of justice was the grimmest of all ironies: it was itself a travesty of justice.

Upon receiving their sentences, the penitents were exhibited to the populace in the *Auto-da-fé*.† Afterwards, stripped to the waist, mounted upon asses, and bearing round their necks inscriptions indicating their offences and the sentences meted out to them, they were whipped through the streets. The Inquisitors showed no mercy either for sex or age. Males or females, old or young, they were all scourged mercilessly. "In the Valencia *Auto* of January 7, 1607," says Lea, "Isabel Madalina Conteri, a Morisca girl of 13, after overcoming torture, had a hundred lashes, Jayme Chulayla, a Morisca of 76, who had been tortured, had a hundred, and the same was administered to Francisco Marquino, aged 86, for sorcery in treasure-secking, while Magdalena Cahet, aged 60, who had escaped torture on account of heart disease, was not spared a hundred."‡

According to Marchant, author of the *History of the Inquisi-*

---

* In Britain the last execution of a heretic was in the year 1696 at Edinburgh.

† The *Auto-da-fé* (Act of Faith) was the term used to describe the ceremony pronouncing or exhibiting the judgment of the Spanish Inquisitors; and (2) the execution of that judgment by the civil authorities. Usually such executions were carried out on a Sunday and were occasions for great rejoicing on the part of the populace.

‡ Henry Charles Lea, *A History of the Inquisition of Spain*, Macmillan, New York, 1906, Vol. III, p. 137.

tion, for saying "I do not know whether the Pope is a man or a woman, and I hear wonderful things of him every day, and I do imagine he must be an animal very rare," a lady was whipped to such a degree that she died a few days afterwards. Such sentences were daily occurrences. We read in Bachaumont's memoirs: "On the 24th of November 1778, the general tribunal of the Inquisition had a secret meeting, at which Paul Olivares appeared, accused of heresy, condemned to confiscation of his property, eight years imprisonment in a monastery, flogged while the psalm Miserere was chanted by assistant priests."

For five hundred years this 'Holy' Inquisition continued in its course of torture, cruelty and persecution. In Spain it reached its apogee, creating records of torture which made the Spanish Inquisition something to be dreaded in all parts of the then known world. Llorente, a contemporary historian, securing his evidence from the records kept by the council of the Inquisition itself, states that in Spain alone, over a period of less than forty years (1481-1517) some 13,000 human beings were burnt at the stake, and that from 1481-1808 the number of persons burnt or tortured reached the colossal total of 341,021. Little wonder that the Roman Catholic faith flourished apace in Europe; little wonder that its power and influence extended with the rapidity of a cyclone!

It was Napoleon who abolished the Spanish Inquisition— one action, at any rate, in his career of bloodshed which one can greet with resounding hosannas. True, this was not the end of it. With the fall of Napoleon from power in 1814, Ferdinand VII was quick to set the Inquisition functioning again, though now shorn of most of its power. But his sadistic triumph was short-lived. In 1820, following the Liberal revolution, the Inquisition was once more suppressed, only to flare up again some five years later. Finally, in 1834, Queen Christina extirpated the cancer for good and all. In Italy, the stronghold of the Popes, it continued to flourish, but it was an emasculated Inquisition and its teeth had been drawn. The days of wholesale and revolting physical torture were gone.

There are, however, other forms of persecution, other forms of torture, other forms of punishment, apart from those introduced, countenanced and practised by the 'Holy' Inquisition, and which represent an Inquisition in fact if not in name. From the beginning of time authors have always had a sword hanging over their heads: they have written the truth at the risk of torture, punishment, and, on occasion, even death. Sylla ordained that writers guilty of libel should suffer the extreme penalty. According to Horace, there was a law which threatened with the bastinado anyone who put into writing a statement decrying a Roman citizen; and because of this law, says Horace, "our satirists changed their style, and for fear of the stick, they said no evil of anyone, and wrote only agreeable verses". And thus through the ages. The rich and the powerful pursued their ways secure in the knowledge that they could punish or imprison any who elected to expose them. Occasionally, of course, someone dared. And inevitably he paid the penalty. Inevitably he suffered martyrdom. For writing *The Marriage of Figaro*, Beaumarchais was flagellated every morning during his confinement in the prison of Saint Lazare. This on the orders of Louis XV. Samuel Johnson, accused of libel, was beaten all the way from Newgate to Tyburn, getting, in all, 317 stripes from a nine-thonged whip. Even Voltaire was flogged. Little wonder that records of the evils of the age were mostly posthumous and rare enough at that.

The Churches, Catholic and Protestant, with the changing of the times and the spreading of more so-called humanitarian reactions, may have had to restrict and revise their methods of persecution. But they have held on to them as long as possible; they were practising their tortures and persecutions until quite recent years, as time goes. Thus, in broad-minded and tolerant England, we find a specimen of religious persecution upheld by the State, which, in its cruelty and intolerance, stinks to heaven. In 1883, at the Central Criminal Court, London, G. W. Foote, then editor of *The Freethinker*, for the publication of criticisms of the Bible, was sentenced by Mr Justice North to twelve months' hard labour. In the face of such a monstrously unjust sentence, well might Foote contemptuously say to the Judge, "My Lord, I thank you—it is worthy of your creed."

This, someone may remark, was over eighty years ago. True. Let us jump forty years or so and come to 1921. In that year, Mr Justice Avory* sentenced a man named Gott to nine months' hard labour for publishing a pamphlet in which he stated that Christ entered Jerusalem "like a circus clown on the back of two donkeys". An appeal against the sentence was dismissed.

During the past forty years, and especially since the Second World War, we have witnessed the development of greater toleration and freedom of expression in many realms of literature, particularly in the fields of Biblical criticism and of sex. But prejudice, resentment and fanaticism still abound, ready to rear their ugly countenance if public opinion will permit it. Even in 1967 one of the Beatles got himself and his group into trouble for having made the perfectly true, if indiscreet assertion that among the younger generation today the Beatles are better known than Jesus Christ. Whipped up by a sensation-loving world Press there was much indignation aroused, in England and the United States, and it was very obvious that quite a number of people would willingly have sentenced the Beatles' spokesman, if not the whole group, to be horse-whipped or jailed, or both . . . And the arbitrariness of censorship in the matter of what is or is not obscene is something that must be encountered to be believed.

---

* It is worthy of note, and not unmixed with a sort of macabre humour, that at the *Freethinker* trial of 1883, Horace Avory (afterwards Mr Justice Avory) was briefed to defend Kemp, one of the co-defendants with Foote.

XIII: CONFESSORS AND FLAGELLATION

THE submission to discipline as a punishment for various misdemeanours in monasteries and convents, and by members of the Church as an atonement, led, not unnaturally, to priests prescribing flagellation as a penance for those confessing their sins. The penitents were told to strip, and to allow themselves to be beaten. Rarely did anyone, rich or poor, refuse the priest's command. Even Saint Louis submitted to the discipline at the hands of his confessors.

The practice was by no means restricted to male penitents. Females similarly were ordered to strip themselves and prepare for the discipline.

As was to be expected, the flogging of female penitents, especially if they were young and not without charm, led to abuses. The priests were eager and ready to prescribe whipping for the remission of all sins and of every sin, and they were even more eager and even more willing to wield the rod themselves upon the naked bodies of the penitents. So much so was this the case, and so keen were priests of the confessional to use the whip, that again and again was it found necessary for the Church to issue regulations designed to curb these appetites and to provide some sort of safeguard. As early in the history of the Church as the time of Pope Adrian I, bishops, priests and deacons were actually forbidden to beat their penitents. Other regulations urged upon priests were the advisability, when hearing the confession of a woman, of having quotations from the Psalms and from other books of the Bible pasted up before their eyes; and of avoiding the concupiscence which privacy might induce, by leaving the doors open.

Despite all precautions, all rules, and all regulations, however, the priests did not hesitate to direct the woman penitent to remove her clothes, a procedure which could not fail to arouse libidinous desires, irrespective of the erotic effects which often resulted from the use of the whip itself.

This offence, on the part of confessors, was classed and punished with that of seduction. Lea mentions an early case of this nature which occurred in 1606. A forty-year-old widow named Maria Escudero testified that her confessor arranged to visit her at her own home "when they would discipline each other with exposure almost complete, under agreement that their eyes should be kept closed".* And in 1795, Padre Paulino Vicente Arévalo, priest of Yepes, was tried and sentenced as "solicitante y flagelante" on his own confession of being guilty of "most flagrant indecencies committed with his female penitents".†

One of the most notorious of the confessors who made a practice of flagellating female penitents was Cornelius Adriasen. It was through his persistent partiality for administering whippings to females that this particular form of discipline came to be generally known as the Cornelian discipline.

In another chapter we shall have occasion to study in some detail the influence of flagellation in arousing eroticism in both the whipper and the whipped, but suffice it to say here that there can be no doubt that the priests, in very considerable numbers, abused their positions and were found guilty of offences against both the men and the women who submitted themselves to the measures imposed in the name of discipline; and there is little doubt, too, that the confessional was often enough a mere excuse for the holding of orgies such as one would expect to find in a brothel.

The fact that exposures were remarkably rare is no evidence whatever that cases were similarly rare. The priests who acted as father confessors had great advantages in respect of licen-

* Henry Charles Lea, *A History of the Inquisition of Spain.*
† *Ibid.*

tious behaviour; and the Church has always hushed up or suppressed, in every possible way, and by every means in its power, anything involving, or casting aspersions on, the morals of the cloth. There are, however, a few cases in the annals of Church history that it has been impossible to suppress; and which are typical of many which have never come to light. One such, known as the Cadière case, is, in fact, so significant that it will prove of value and interest to give it a brief examination here.

The *dramatis personae* immediately concerned in what proved to be one of the most sensational cases ever to come before an ecclesiastical court, were Catherine Cadière, a beautiful twenty-five-year-old girl of well-to-do parents, and Jean-Baptiste Girard, a fifty-year-old Jesuit priest. The scene was Toulon. In 1728 Father Girard, who previously had been a priest at Aix-la-Chapelle, was transferred to Toulon, where Mademoiselle Cadière resided. The priest proved immensely popular, especially with the women, and his confessions were attended by all the girls and young ladies in the neighbourhood. In all of which there was nothing unusual. But the priest was fifty, a dangerous age, and he was accustomed to administer what the Church euphemistically described as "the discipline" to his penitents. For a priest of fifty years to listen to the erotic confessions of charming young ladies is dangerous enough, but when, in addition, he witnesses them disrobing, and when, further, he uses a whip on their naked posteriors, the whole thing becomes more than dangerous—it verges on the catastrophic. At any rate, the charming Cadière girl became one of his penitents, or pupils, as he preferred to call them, and there can be no doubt that he gained a good deal of influence over her, bringing to his aid, according to the girl's allegations, sorcery and witchcraft. Whether, as was alleged at the subsequent inquiry, Catherine set herself deliberately to infatuate the Father, or whether the priest just as deliberately plotted and planned to seduce the girl, was never quite cleared up, as there was undoubtedly a good deal of perjury, evasion and subterfuge on both sides, but probably there was blameworthy conduct on the part of both priest and penitent. What, however, became sufficiently clear was that Father Girard, a man old enough to be the girl's father in fact as well as fancy, gave to her a tremendous amount of attention, visited her at her home, whipped her there to his heart's content, and had sexual intercourse with her. So great and so regular were his attentions that talk and suspicion were aroused, and the Father found himself in danger of having to stop his visits to the Cadière home. The next chapter in the story sees Catherine, at Girard's suggestion, entering the convent of Ollioules as a nun, where, in his capacity of priest, Father Girard was able to visit her regularly and administer 'the discipline'. Now, whether the girl tired of the priest's attentions, or whether, as seems more probable, he went from bad to worse, until his 'discipline' became of a nature such as no girl possessing the slightest shreds of decency could possibly stand, is not clear; but in the end Catherine complained to, and poured the whole story into the ears of, the Bishop of Toulon. Father Girard was suspended, and, after much discussion and protracted inquiries, the matter came before the High Court of Justice at Aix. It proved a *cause célèbre*. The Society of Jesuits, who looked upon the whole affair as a reflection upon the Brotherhood, and damaging to their cause, fought tooth and nail in Father Girard's defence. The girl, to her considerable consternation, I fancy, found herself treated like a criminal. She was threatened in a dozen ways; she was accused of perjury, of conspiracy, and worse. And, in the end, the jury could not agree and the case was dismissed.

An equally notorious instance was that of the Franciscan monk, Cornelius Hadrien, who was attached to a convent at Bruges, and for ten years, from 1548 to 1558, succeeded in covering with the cloak of religion a life of sexual debauchery and perversity that would take some surpassing even in the case-histories of the psycho-analysts. His method was carefully thought out, and I have no doubt was considered by the priest himself to be foolproof. To certain of the girls who attended the confessional he suggested that, with their parents' consent, they should visit his house, which adjoined the convent, once a week in order to be given special and necessary private instruction in 'holy obedience'. With scarcely an exception, as was to be expected, the parents gave their consent, for Hadrien ranked as a theologian of the most distinguished order. The girls discovered that the 'instruction' included what the priest termed 'private discipline', and which, in plain English, meant the application of the whip to their naked bodies. His pupils included a number of ladies of high rank, and seeing that the game went on every week and merrily for ten whole years before exposure came, it would appear that most of these pupils enjoyed it as much perhaps as did their libidinous tutor.

PART FOUR

THE CASE FOR AND AGAINST CORPORAL PUNISHMENT

XIV: THE PSYCHOLOGY OF PUNISHMENT

PAIN, physical or mental, is the essence of punishment. Every form of punishment that has been devised has had for its object the infliction of pain or suffering upon the individual; physical pain in some cases, psychical suffering in others, a combination of physical pain and mental suffering in most.

The earliest of all forms of punishment was neither more nor less than private vengeance, immortalised in the proverb "An eye for an eye, a tooth for a tooth". Often this was tantamount to retaliation—that precise form of punishment which, in essence, consists in the retribution or revenge which one person metes out to an enemy, and which is analogous to the destructive vengeance which one animal inflicts upon another.

The next step in the evolution of a punitive system was exemplified in the putting upon the tribal god or gods the responsibility for the infliction of punishment. This was common to all primitive and savage races which had emerged from pure animism. The wishes of the gods were interpreted by the magicians and priests of the tribes.

With the advent and growth of civilisation the whole concept of punishment was elaborated and the responsibility for its ordering and its infliction was no longer placed upon God, but was accepted by society itself. With this new development the number of violations of rules and the need for retributive or punitive measures has enormously extended. The machinery for inflicting punishment became ever more extensive.

It has always been difficult for the unprejudiced onlooker to decide where and in what circumstances punishment becomes torture. In many cases the two terms are synonymous. Often what one individual would call a just form of punishment another would term torture. In many cases the actual punishment which society imposed was preceded by torture. Often the preliminary torture to which the culprit was subjected alone rendered possible the imposition of any form of prescribed punishment at all. Indeed, the need for this preliminary system of torture was inseparable from the growth of a system of punishment elaborated by society as a just measure of protection. Such a system implied, as its basic essentiality, the proof of guilt. It was the need to prove the guilt of the accused, in accordance with society's concept of justice, that caused confession to be looked upon as the primary need. Confession was the finest possible evidence of guilt, and it was with the express object of securing this irrefutable evidence, that in both the ecclesiastical and civil courts, for century after century of the Christian era, every effort was made to induce the accused to admit guilt. Practically the only way in which any such confession could be secured was by torture. In the witchcraft trials of the Middle Ages every form of torture human ingenuity could devise was employed to this end. The monsters who acted as Inquisitors brought torture to a fine art.

In modern civilisation torture is *supposedly* abhorrent to the humanitarianism which is conceded to be part and parcel of the punitive system. The punishment which is inherent in the penal system of every civilised country today is acclaimed to be humane and just. As such it is held to be in no sense of the word torture. The dissociation of torture from punishment is not easy, however. So long as those associated with the protection of society from its marauders are rewarded for the punishment of crime rather than its prevention; and so long as the nature and degree of the punishment are decided by the nature of the crime rather than the psychology of the criminal, it is impossible to dissociate, in any complete or adequate sense, torture from punishment.

For centuries punishment was concerned solely with exacting

vengeance and deterring potential or actual criminals from committing or repeating offences against society. While the deterrent object still figures largely in every penal code, there has been added, as a contemporary and subsidiary objective, the reformation of the criminal himself where such reformation is held to be possible or desirable in the interests of the State.

The need for or the desirability of reform has led to changes in the whole concept of punishment. There are certain modes of punishment which are directly opposed to the reform of the individual criminal, in many instances leading to a repetition of the offence and the development of a confirmed criminal or anti-social outlook. On the other hand, the humanitarians, in their reformative zeal, are inclined to overlook one of the primary objects of punishment, i.e. the deterrent effect which, by force of example, it is held to have upon the rest of the community.

The popular concept that the criminal is necessarily an abnormal individual, restricted to certain hereditary types or to a certain social stratum, may be a comforting theory, but it is a fallacious one. Every individual is a potential criminal. The avoidance of crime is not due, in the vast majority of instances, to the possession of any high moral principles. On the contrary, it is due to the fear of exposure, of ostracism or of punishment. The only crime, in the final, and ultimate, analysis, is the crime of being found out. And if the punishment of crime ever becomes of such a nature that it carries with it no degree of ostracism, shame, interference with liberty, or heavy financial loss, it ceases to act in any way as a deterrent. In addition, the crime itself diminishes coincidentally in seriousness. The serious crime of one century becomes the merest peccadillo in another.

The stealing of property of any description is an offence punishable by imprisonment. But actually the punishment does not end with the serving of the term of imprisonment. There is also involved social ostracism and, in certain cases, a perpetual sense of shame. The injury to another individual or to his property, committed by a drunken or an incapable motorist is an offence punishable by the paying of monetary compensation and, in certain cases, by a fine. But here the matter ends. There is no sense of shame involved, there is no such a thing as social ostracism. Moreover, the motorist can insure against his liability, in other words, against his punishment. The result is that this punishment has no deterrent action either against the repetition of the offence by the same individual or its commission by another. Here we touch upon a phase of modern society's reaction to the offences against its ordinances which resembles closely that which held force in primitive races where the punishment meted out constituted a full discharge of the criminal's debt to society, and the offender, provided he escaped the death penalty, was free to repeat his acts.

In modern civilisation the deterrent power of the punishment meted out for any given crime against society is governed by the chances of that crime being discovered and the culprit detected. Especially is this true in regard to the professional criminal. If the risk of detection is so remote as to be negligible, the punishment, whatever its nature or extent may be, loses so much of its deterrent or remedial value as to cease to justify its existence as a form of punishment. It becomes merely a measure of vengeance and, as such, is unjustifiable and inexcusable.

The effects of punishment are governed by the nature of the individual who is punished. It is because of this that punishment as a reformative agent is often valueless. It is nearly always valueless in the case of the professional criminal, and in the case of a pervert or other abnormal individual who commits a criminal act. It is invariably useless in the case of a maniac who turns to crime. The only effective method in such cases is segregation as a protective or restrictive measure.

In all cases where punishment may have a reformative effect, the danger lies in an error being made in the nature or extent of the form of punishment decreed by the law. Often severe or degrading forms of punishment defeat all possible hopes of reformation. Instead, a habitual or professional criminal may be created.

It is here that the importance arises of the nature of the punishment being decreed, not so much by the criminal act itself as by the cause of the crime and the psychology of the criminal. An offence, or even a grave crime, may be induced by thoughtlessness or carelessness. In another instance, a similar crime may be deliberately performed because of the pleasure which the individual derives from the commission of the crime. To adopt the same punishment in both cases is largely to defeat any reformative and preventive effects which punishment may be held to possess.

Exceptionally severe or brutal punishment is a certain preventive of reform. It negates any justification which punishment may be held to possess. There is no doubt that, in numberless instances, punishment, through its needless severity, has turned the accidental into the habitual criminal. The story of Ira Marlatt, the 'demon' of the Ohio State Penitentiary, is an example of what terrible results excessive punishment and callous treatment may bring in their train. This convict Marlatt made some complaint or other to one of the guards, and, in consequence, was accused of 'insolence' and paddled. Now Marlatt was a man of phenomenal physical strength, blessed with an iron constitution, and possessing the will to rebel against what he thought to be an injustice. He refused to work as a protest against the treatment meted out to him. The prison officials, in their determination to break Marlatt's spirit, used every form of torture the regulations allowed. They beat him from head to foot with 'sanded' paddles; they used the bull rings and the 'water cure'. But they could not break him. He fought like a maniac, disabling several of the warders. Finally, on the grounds of being a dangerous madman, Marlatt was imprisoned like a wild beast in a steel enclosure known as the 'demon's cage'. And, truth to tell, as a result of this treatment, the convict had all the appearance of a savage ape-man. He gibbered at officials and visitors alike when they approached his cage, and, on one occasion, when a warder ventured too near the bars, Marlatt stretched out a vengeful hand, armed with a sharp piece of metal, and slit the guard's face from side to side.

The years went their way, and Ira Marlatt, like the wild beast men had made him, lived in his iron cage. Then, says Charles Edward Russell, to whom I am indebted for the facts of this remarkable affair,

"One day Senator Rose, of Marietta, a noted public man and new member of the Board of Prison Managers, came to the penitentiary and asked about Marlatt, of whose case he had heard so much. They showed him the Demon's cage. He asked for the key. There was a volume of protest. The senator was assured that to go near Marlatt was equivalent to committing suicide. But Senator Rose persisted and the door was opened. The visitor advanced with outstretched hand. 'Come, Marlatt,' he said, 'let's be friends.' The Demon took the proffered hand and shook it. 'Now,' said Mr Rose, 'let's sit down here. I want to talk with you.' They sat down side by side, and for half an hour talked quietly. It was the first time anyone had spoken decently to the convict or looked upon him with any but a menacing countenance. All his life he had been accustomed to blows and curses, and had given the like blows and curses to others. No one had ever offered him a hand nor a kindly word. So now as they sat there and talked he seemed strangely moved. When they got up, they walked out and sought the warden. 'This man wants to go to work,' said Mr Rose. From that time on there was no more trouble with Marlatt. He never afterwards occupied the Demon's cage nor received any other punishment. You can see him in the prison now. He is one of the trusties, janitor of the hospital, a model prisoner."*

* Quoted in *Prison Reform*, pp. 61-2, from an article by Charles Edward Russell in *Hampton's Magazine*, October, 1909.

XV: PHYSICAL AND PSYCHOLOGICAL EFFECTS OF WHIPPING ADULTS

WE have seen that the justification for any form of punishment other than that of segregation or confinement as a purely preventive measure, lies in its value as a reformative or deterrent agent.

The question arises of how far the administration of corporal punishment achieves the one object or the other.

The point has been hotly and repeatedly debated. From the beginning of civilisation there have abounded those who have strenuously advocated the employment and extolled the virtues of corporal punishment just as there have been those who denounced it as barbarous, cruel and ineffectual.

There have, too, been 'waves' of public opinion in favour of flogging, usually as a result of the outbreak of a spate of some particular crime, and especially in connexion with sexual or moral offences. The garrotting outbreak in 1862 led to the demand for the use of the 'cat' in all cases of 'robbery with violence'; and, half a century later, the 'white slavery' scare caused the passing of the Criminal Law Amendment Act of 1912, which sanctioned the flogging of those found guilty of participation in the immoral traffic.

It is contended by some authorities on criminology that corporal punishment is more effective than are most of the penalties which have supplanted it, and, at the same time, is not productive of such lasting or permanent injuries to the mind. The argument is that the ill-effects of flogging, provided always it is reasonable in its extent and in its severity, are restricted to a few days; the effects of solitary confinement, or of the mental tortures connected with modern 'third degree' methods, may well have psychological results the extent of which it is impossible to anticipate. A further contention is that the present-day horror of anything which smacks of physical pain has brought in its train a tendency to substitute modes of punishment which are, in many cases, psychologically injurious to the convicted person, while they provide no means of deterring others from committing similar crimes. In other cases a fine is the only form of punishment inflicted.

To very many persons a fine does not constitute any punishment at all. To impose any ordinary fine on a prosperous individual and imagine that it is a punishment borders on the farcical; the most it can do is to cause some slight annoyance. In many cases it does not even annoy. And for this reason it does not, in the majority of cases, act as a deterrent.

The effects of flogging are, however, in the majority of instances, far from being of the transitory and superficial nature that many of its advocates would have us believe. And these effects vary very considerably in their nature according to the physiology and psychology of the individual. In numerous cases, as we have seen (notably Chapters V and VII), diseases of a serious nature, and even death itself, may follow severe floggings; and although in these modern days, under medical supervision, there is perhaps no risk to life itself, there may easily be induced certain disorders as direct results of such floggings.

Very nearly a couple of centuries ago some notion of these dangers to physical health had been grasped by the medical practitioners of that age. In *The History of the Flagellants* (1777) we read:

"In fact, Physicians and Anatomists inform us, that such is the secret of open communication between all parts of the human body, that it is impossible to do any material and continued kind of injury to any one without other parts being sooner or later affected by it: hence it results that those persons

136

who execute disciplines upon themselves with the great severity we mention, in time fall into some serious disorders of one kind or other, and at last find themselves disabled from continuing any longer a practice which was so useful to the improvement of their morals."

We have seen that Private Somerville attributed the illness which followed his flogging to the effects of the punishment he received (Chapter VII) and there can be little doubt that this suspicion was a correct one.

Writing in *The Humanitarian* (July, 1905) Dr Alexander Haig pointed out that the pain incidental to flogging "raises the blood pressure", and this in turn throws increased work upon the heart. The strain thus produced results in the heart never being quite the same again;* and Dr Marshall Hall says: "I assert from positive knowledge that each lash goes literally to the very heart, paralysing or enfeebling its action."†

Bad, however, as are the physical effects of the 'cat', the psychological effects, in most cases, are very much more serious. It is doubtful if flogging can ever in any circumstances prove to be a reformative agent. In this respect it fails with the professional and hardened criminal as it does with the first offender. The professional criminal cannot be reformed. Nor can the pathological case. "Some time ago," says George Ives, "I received a letter from an eminent criminal lawyer in Melbourne alluding to a prisoner who had five times been flogged for five separate sexual offences."‡

In the case of the first offender not only does flogging, in nine cases out of ten, fail to prevent a repetition of the offence, it nearly always succeeds effectually in ensuring such a repetition. The very type of individual who is the most likely to respond to treatment destined to bring about his reform is sure to be turned, by a dose of the 'cat', into an enemy of society, a bitter, disgraced, degraded outcast.

* Quoted by Henry S. Salt in *The Flogging Craze*.
† *Ibid.*
‡ George Ives, *A History of Penal Methods*, Stanley Paul, 1914, p. 351.

The late Mr Justice Mathew said: "I believe that if a man has any good in him, and is punished with the 'cat', he is either for the rest of his days a broken-hearted man, or he becomes a reckless criminal"; and Mr Justice Hawkins affirmed: "You make a perfect devil of the man you flog."*

Does the 'cat' act as a preventive of crime by deterring any criminal from repeating his offence or a potential criminal from committing a first offence? Here again we are confronted with the fact that individuals vary very considerably in their reaction to different forms of punishment. According to Colonel Baker of the Salvation Army, there are some prisoners who "would rather go to the lash than into solitary confinement"; and Mr George Ives, to whom I am indebted for this opinion of the Colonel's, states that the Governor of an Australian prison told him "that one rather troublesome convict, whom he had placed by himself to keep him away from the rest, had petitioned that he might receive a flogging if only he might then rejoin them".† In the case of the hardened habitual criminal flogging will prove no deterrent, for here we are concerned with a man who has deliberately chosen a criminal profession and who is prepared to pay the penalty should he be caught. The punishment he receives is his payment for the debt he owes society; the ordeal over, he starts again on his career of crime. In this connexion the remarks of Governor Macquarie are revealing:

"If flogging is efficacious in preventing crime, it should have made the convict colonies the most virtuous places on earth, for the 'cat' was in almost continuous use in New South Wales and in Van Dieman's Land. The 'cat' generally used was the ordinary military or naval 'cat'; but the 'cat' used at Macquarie Harbour was a larger and heavier instrument than that used generally for the punishment of soldiers or sailors. It was called the thief's 'cat', or double cat-o'-nine-tails. It had only the usual number of tails, but each of these was a double twist of

* Henry S. Salt, *The Flogging Craze.*
† George Ives, *A History of Penal Methods*, p. 227.

138

whipcord, and each tail had nine knots. It was a very formidable instrument indeed."*

"How far," says Boxall in commenting on the Governor's statement, "the influence of this barbarous instrument of torture tended to make the prisoners at Macquarie Harbour the most reckless and ferocious of the convicts of Australia it is unnecessary to enquire, but there can be no doubt that its influence was for evil and not for good."

With the man who, through thoughtlessness, in a mad gust of rage, as a result of a pathological state, or other transient condition, commits a crime, the matter is on an entirely different footing. In such a case a flogging will surely prove useless as a preventive of any repetition of the offence, as in most respects the circumstances are not likely to arise where a repetition of the crime is feasible or probable, and in other cases, owing purely to pathological conditions, any form of punishment will prove unavailing. What is most likely is that in the case of any individual whose reform is possible, a flogging will merely succeed in turning him into a hardened criminal.

Flogging with the 'cat', by its very severity, may prove a factor in increasing crime. As Beccaria truly says: "The very severity of a punishment leads men to dare so much the more to escape it, according to the greatness of the evil in prospect; and many crimes are thus committed to avoid the penalty of a single one."† Once a man has suffered the tortures of flogging, the possibility of a repetition of the punishment may easily cause the commission of a far more serious crime in an effort to escape such punishment.

One of the main arguments advanced by those in favour of flogging is that the dread of the ordeal is sufficient, in itself, to

* Dispatch from Governor Macquarie to Earl Bathurst (June 28, 1813) quoted by George E. Boxall in *History of the Australian Bushrangers*, pp. 4-5.

† James Anson Farrer, *Crimes and Punishments, including a new Translation of Beccaria's "Dei Delitti e delle Pene"*, Chatto & Windus, 1880, p. 167.

deter others from committing an offence punishable by flogging. It is thus held to be an excellent preventive of crime. No
doubt the argument was, in some respects, a sound one in those
days when floggings were carried out in full view of the public.
But with the prohibition of public flogging the deterrent value
of this form of punishment has been shorn of nearly all its
potency.

Finally, there is to be considered the *effect of flogging upon the
person wielding the 'cat'*, a point this which seems rarely to be
taken into account. Unless the flogger is a sadist or a man
devoid of all humanitarian feeling, the task must be a revolting
and debasing one. However much he may denounce the
offence for which the prisoner is to be punished he finds the
infliction of the punishment a most distasteful affair. It is one
thing to thrash a man in a moment of passion at the time an
offence is committed; it is entirely another thing to flog that
individual in cold blood when he is tied up and defenceless,
and long after the commission of the offence.

In this connexion, the personal impressions of John Shipp,
of the 87th Foot Regiment, who had himself inflicted many
floggings, are of vital interest and significance. He says:

"From the very first day I entered the service as drum-boy,
and for eight years after, I can venture to assert that, at the
lowest calculation, it was my disgusting duty to flog men at
least three times a week. From this painful task there was no
possibility of shrinking, without the certainty of a rattan over
my own shoulders by the drum-major, or of my being sent to
the black-hole. When the infliction is ordered to commence,
each drum-boy, in rotation, is obliged to strip, for the purpose
of administering five-and-twenty lashes (slowly counted by
the drum-major), with freedom and vigour. In this practice
of stripping there always appeared to me something so un-
natural, inhuman, and butcher-like, that I have often felt most
acutely my own degradation in being compelled to conform to
it. After a poor fellow had received about a hundred lashes the
blood would fly down his back in streams, and fly about in all

directions with every additional blow of the instrument of torture; so that by the time he had received 300, I have found my clothes all over blood from the knees to the crown of my head, and have looked as though I had just emerged from the slaughter-house. Horrified at my disgusting appearance, immediately after parade I have run into the barrack-room to escape from the observation of the soldiers, and to rid my clothes of my comrade's blood. Here I have picked and washed off my clothes pieces of skin and flesh that had been cut from the poor sufferer's back."*

Commenting upon the futility of corporal punishment as a means of maintaining prison discipline, Mr Compton Mackenzie wrote:

"If men were allowed to smoke from the beginning of their sentence, and if breaches of discipline were punished by deprivation of smoking, the cat might become a museum piece with the scold's bridle and the thumbscrews. Not much over a hundred years ago a woman was flogged through the streets of Inverness. Nowadays we cannot understand the mental processes of great-grandparents who allowed such a display of barbarism. A hundred years hence our own mental processes which allow the cat-o'-nine-tails to be used in prisons will be equally unimaginable."†

* John Shipp, *Flogging and Its Substitute*, London, 1831, p. 20.
† Compton Mackenzie in *Walls Have Mouths, A Record of Ten Years' Penal Servitude*, by Wilfred Macartney, Gollancz, 1936, p. 170.

XVI: PHYSICAL AND PSYCHOLOGICAL EFFECTS
OF JUVENILE BIRCHING

ADMITTEDLY there is a considerable gulf between the flogging of an adult with the 'cat' and the thrashing of a youngster with the birch-rod, although both species of castigation come within the category of corporal punishment. There is no danger to life and limb in a birching inflicted under proper supervision, and rarely is such a castigation followed by any deleterious effects upon the delinquent's physical health. The dangers and evils connected with it are of quite another character.

The problem of dealing with juvenile offences is a difficult one. It is difficult because here the field of punishment is necessarily very much restricted. Imprisonment and fines, two of the most widely employed methods for dealing with all but major offences of adults, are ruled out altogether.* Segregation in reformatories is not always practicable, and in certain cases it does not constitute a form of punishment possessing reformative or deterrent characteristics.

It is for these reasons that many persons, including judges in both England and America, hold the opinion that whipping, especially of young offenders, would have a salutary effect. In America, two Kansas judges, according to a report in the *New York Herald Tribune* (March 11, 1928), stated: "Unless the punishment is accomplished in a cruel and unusual manner, high school girls who receive whippings at home will not find

* The imprisonment of children was, however, abolished only in 1908 in England.

142

redress in the courts of this country"; and another judge's "answer to many who called him on the telephone to find out what they could have recourse to if they had children who needed to be disciplined was 'Give them whippings.' He stated that he knew at least 150 girls in the city (Kansas City) who deserved good whippings. Most of them, he said, are between 11 and 16 years old."* In 1935, according to a report in the *News of the World*, a judge in sentencing a youth of eighteen years to six months' imprisonment on three charges of theft, said: "If I were at liberty to do as I think best for you, I should order you to be well whipped, but I have no power to do that."†

Superintendent H. Rigby, in commenting upon the growth of juvenile crime in the town of Wigan, said: "I want to suggest quite seriously that the method of dealing with juveniles under the Act has proved a complete failure. Other remedies will have to be found. I have never known of a juvenile who has had the birch and returned."‡

At the 1937 Conference of the British Medical Association at Belfast, Dr H. Rose said that "in 30 years he had not seen any ill effects from the birching of children", while Dr Gilbert Orme, "ex-school medical officer to one of England's big public schools", stated that "there were certain children with such a character that there was only one way of dealing with them, and that was to administer judicial punishment".

A South African clergyman, the Rev. T. B. Powell, in an address to the East London (South Africa) Rotary Club, stated that he

"considered that in homes and schools there should be a greater use of the rod and said that discipline generally, and more particularly discipline in the home, in every South African town, was at a very low ebb. Discipline had played an important part in the building up of every big nation and he stressed

---

* Quoted in *The Strap Returns: New Notes on Flagellation*, The Gargoyle Press, New York, privately printed, 1933.

† *News of the World*, June 23, 1935.

‡ *Daily Herald*, June 30, 1937.

the value and usefulness of the discipline in the old Greek State of Sparta. There youths had been thrashed, not because they had done wrong but for the good of their souls, and it had proved of great value to the boys and to the world."*

Pro-flogging views are still being expressed in judicial quarters today. Mr Reginald Seaton, chairman of the Inner London Sessions, was quoted in 1967 as saying: "I had my first touch of the stick, if I remember rightly, within seven days at school; for throwing bread. I do agree with corporal punishment, I think it's a great pity that the birch isn't permissible today. People always feared corporal punishment."†

In contradistinction to these views is a formidable array of opinion against whipping of every description as a punitive measure.

When the question of the birching of juveniles was discussed at the 1937 meeting of the British Medical Association, previously mentioned, the consensus of opinion was in fact that the practice should be abolished. Dr W. N. Maple said: "I have not met one person who specializes in child psychology who does not say that birching is responsible for infinite harm"; while in the opinion of Dr P. B. Spurgin "birching was a barbarous thing. Judicial birching, in his opinion, was not only unnecessary but was likely to be disastrous to the future of juvenile delinquents so treated"; and Dr Nunan, speaking "as one who has witnessed judicial birching, said the effect it left on his mind was that it was revolting, degrading, and inhuman".

In an address to the Birmingham Trades Council on "Juvenile Delinquency and the Work of the Juvenile Courts", Mr George Haynes, a magistrate who, as a boy, had been birched at school himself, stated: " 'I am not ashamed to say that I have had experience by a dose of the birch. I have also witnessed a birching—the whole school watched a boy receiving corporal punishment from the headmaster. They were

* *Natal Mercury*, June 4, 1937.
† *Sunday Times*, November 5, 1967.

terrifying experiences.' Mr Haynes was quite satisfied in his own mind that corporal punishment was not good," and went on to say that " 'it should also be realised that whereas years ago the birching was done almost immediately, nowadays 24 hours might elapse—waiting for medical examination, etc.—before the punishment was inflicted. In the meantime parents and child were in mental torment.' "*

"You can whip vice into a boy, but you can't whip it out," was the opinion of Mr Walter Parsons, Chairman of Leeds Juvenile Court for a number of years in the 'thirties, who might fairly claim to have had some experience in the treatment of juvenile delinquents. "Further," said Mr Parsons, "psychologists are more and more playing a part in the work of juvenile courts. And as the psychologist comes in, the birch goes out."†

In a thoughtful article on "The Birching of Children" in the *British Medical Journal* (March 20, 1937) appeared the following passage:

"A judicial birching, whatever may be the injury to the mind of a growing human being, might well confirm the offender in his potentially criminal ways. The aim should not be to punish the delinquent but to discover what social, familial and personal factors are responsible for his anti-social tendencies and to institute treatment to correct them. To tie him hand and foot to a tripod and flog him with a brine-soaked birch seems the best way to make a boy of 8 years look upon society as his natural enemy."

Before corporal punishment of the young was abolished by law, there was a growing weight of conviction among authoritative opinion that whipping was of little value as a deterrent. The same offender was birched again and again. The late Sir William Clarke Hall, an authority on juvenile crime, discontinued ordering birching as he found a very high percentage

* *Birmingham Gazette*, July 5, 1937.
† *Yorkshire Evening News*, August 4, 1937.

of recidivists among the boys who were whipped, and concluded this form of punishment was of little value.

Cicely M. Craven, the Honorary Secretary of the Howard League, in a letter to the *Oxford Times* (July 30, 1937) wrote:

"The experience of the courts wherever records have been kept systematically of the after-history of boys who have been birched show that the percentage of re-convictions is higher than the corresponding percentage for any other form of treatment by the juvenile court. The Board of Education made a study of all the cases dealt with over a period of years by the courts of four large towns which at that period used the birch freely, i.e. for all sorts of offences and not merely for the 'bad hats'. The facts revealed showed that of all the boys birched, over 25 per cent were re-convicted within one month, and over 76 per cent within two years. No other method had such a startling record of failure."

The main trouble with the corporal punishment of children, as of adults, lies in the dangers connected with any system which overlooks variations in the physical and mental health of the delinquents, and which allots a form of punishment that is so greatly dependent, as regards its severity, on the person who inflicts the punishment. Whether we are considering birching inflicted by parents or others at the moment the offence is committed, or by prison officials under adequate supervision and after an inquiry, matters little.

The degree of punishment which may have no deleterious physical effects in the case of a normal child, may lead to serious illness where a youngster in weak health is concerned. The flogging, light or severe, which may be borne with equanimity or nonchalance by a child already introduced to a life of crime, may, in the case of a first offender, have psychological effects which can never afterwards be eradicated. The danger, in all cases, is that the infliction of corporal punishment will create sullenness, hypocrisy and cunning where these did not previously exist, or that it will develop or extend these undesirable characteristics in all instances where they were already in existence. "In my life's experience," said Mr Justice Du Parcq, "I have always noticed that a judicial child flogging is the first sentence in the tragedy of a life of crime."*

The writer of the article on "Flogging" in the *Encyclopaedia Britannica* (fourteenth edition) with much truth said:

"Modern psychiatry and genetic psychology have shown the dangers inherent in flogging children, in that such procedure may develop inhibitions, antipathies and neurotic traits likely to undermine the whole mental and nervous system of the child."

An instance of such an inhibitory effect is related by William of Malmesbury as long ago as the time of King Ethelred's childhood. The future king was flogged by his mother wi h candles to such effect that the child was driven very nearly frantic. So intense was the impression on his mind, and so closely related was the sight of candles with pain, that during the whole of his future life the King would never allow a candle to be lighted in his presence.

The interval which must necessarily elapse between the commission of the offence and the infliction of a judicial birching detracts considerably from the value of the punishment as a disciplinary and deterring measure, and at the same time increases considerably its possibilities of inflicting psychological harm. A good thrashing delivered at the moment when the offence is committed is something quite different from a flogging administered days or weeks afterwards by a police officer. It is because of this that many of those who still retain some respect for Solomon's oft-quoted maxim consider that in place of judicial birching the infliction of floggings on the instant and on the spot by parents, guardians, teachers and reformatory officials, should be allowed and encouraged. This, it is contended, would overcome the two most potent objections to judicial birchings: namely, that, as already mentioned, too long an interval occurs between the committing of

* Quoted by Dr W. N. Maple in his address to the British Medical Association's Conference, 1937.

147

the offence and the punishment; and that birching by a police-man carries with it a degree of degradation out of all proportion to the gravity of the offence. It is true that the infliction of a sound thrashing immediately after an offence has been committed would seem, particularly in relation to certain offences such as cruelty to other children and to animals, to be most fitting and efficacious; and, at the same time, that such a castigation, from the point of view of the one who inflicts it, being given in the heat of the moment and at a time of virtuous indignation, would be devoid of that cold-bloodedness which is so sinister a feature of judicial floggings. But whatever virtue such a system might possess is grossly outweighed by other dangers inherent in any method which encourages floggings in circumstances where adequate supervision is impossible or unlikely. Also one must not overlook the possibilities opened up, if once the licence to punish is given to parents and teachers, of brutality and sadistic impulses finding scope for indulgence. Finally, the child who has been severely whipped feels that he has a grudge against his persecutors, and this applies not only to police-court and school punishments but also where the father is the wielder of the rod, a point which looms large in any argument against home castigation. There are so many cases where the hatred of a son for his father is due solely to severe thrashings administered during childhood.

In addition to all the dangerous effects of flogging which have already been enumerated, there are certain matters connected with the sexual side which, through ignorance of their existence, few people take into consideration. These evils I shall examine in the next chapter. They are of vital importance as they constitute one of the most powerful arguments against the birching of youngsters in all or in any circumstances.

XVII: EVILS CONNECTED WITH FLOGGING
AND BIRCHING

IT is a well-known fact that flagellation stimulates sexual excitement in certain circumstances. It is true that there are a limited number of references only to erotic flagellation in ancient literature, and this paucity of evidence has led some writers to conclude that whipping for the purpose of sexual excitation is a comparatively modern development, and others to assert that its influence in this direction is restricted to a small number of perverts or pathological cases. I think both these inferences are based upon the most dubious of premises.

The fact that a social phenomenon finds little or no mention in contemporary literature is not in any sense evidential one way or the other. There may be half a dozen cogent and powerful reasons why a feature of the social life of the day receives little comment in contemporary circles. This may happen, and it has happened, in our own day. It was a hundred times more likely to happen during those times when the ancient civilisations were beginning to emerge from their swaddling clothes. The significance of religion's remarkable power must not be overlooked in dealing with any aspect of life before, say, the middle of the nineteenth century. The critic was in danger of losing his liberty, if not his life. The commentator on habits or activities which the Church or the State wished to keep unchronicled was in similar danger (see Chapter XII). Now, bearing these points well in mind, and connecting them with the fact, which has been amply demonstrated in the preceding pages of this work, that flagellation was looked upon as a most useful tool in the hands of the Church—a Church opposed, ostensibly at any rate, tooth and nail to all manifestations of the sexual appetite, and pledged to wage relentless war upon anything likely to arouse or excite this appetite—and we have a powerful and compelling reason for the exercise of a judicious but adequate censorship. Small wonder, therefore, that in all the accounts concerning flagellation in the monasteries and nunneries, there are few references to any sexual stimulatory influence of such flagellation, purposeful or accidental.

The hypothesis that flagellation arouses sexual excitation in certain individuals who are described as perverts, and in these individuals only, while having more foundation in fact than have many other hypotheses advanced, would appear to be partially an exaggeration and partially an attempt to suppress the truth. Certainly the sexual element does not *always* enter into flagellation. By no means. If the punishment is severe, as, for instance, in cases of flogging criminals with the 'cat', there will be, *normally*, no sexual excitement induced in the person flogged, though there may well be a sadistic element present in the executioner or the onlookers. Erotic flagellation, with rare exceptions, is not *severe* flagellation. *Usually*, it will, and can, have no permanent or protracted physically injurious effects. In fact, for the most part, wherever flagellation reaches a degree of severity which can truly cause it to rank as a punishment, it ceases to be erotic, *so far as concerns the person being whipped.** Here any such excitation is restricted to the individual inflicting the punishment and those witnessing its infliction.

In the old days, when floggings and birchings were performed in full view of the public, the sexual element entered into the matter very much more than it does today; especially so when, previous to the beginning of the nineteenth century, it was customary not only to flog females as well as males, but to flog them in public. For, in any consideration of the erotic

* The exceptions, which are not to be overlooked, are those abnormal individuals who secure pleasure from punishment, even severe punishment, inflicted upon their own bodies. There is also a possibility of developing masochistic or sadistic impulses in formerly normal individuals.

effects of flagellation, the sex of the individual receiving the whipping and of the person wielding the whip, both loom large. The whipping of a female, whether under the aegis of religious discipline, an educational curriculum, or a penological system, was brimming with possibilities of sexual excitations. It does not necessarily call for either sadism on the one hand, or masochism on the other, to explain the existence of such phenomena.

There are three different types of persons who find pleasure in flagellation. These are (1) those who take a delight in whipping or punishing others; (2) those who experience pleasure in being whipped; and (3) those who enjoy witnessing the whipping administered to someone else. Apart from a few cases of pure unadulterated love of cruelty for its own sake, all these cases are intimately connected with sex. In many instances there is, in addition, a vicarious sexual pleasure induced by reading detailed descriptions of whippings, and imagining oneself playing some role or other in connexion with such occurrences.

One of the few early references to erotic flagellation is to be found in that classic of Roman debauchery, the *Satyricon* of Petronius, but, no doubt owing to the fact that there is no mention of an actual whip or birch being used, the account has been overlooked or ignored by many writers and historians. According to Petronius, when Encolpus, to his horror and humiliation, found himself stricken with impotence, Oenothea, priestess of Priapus, undertook to effect a cure by means of fustigation with ripe nettles.

In fact there are grounds for the supposition that *urtication*, as that form of flagellation in which nettles were used instead of a whip or stick was termed, achieved considerable popularity among the Romans and other ancient races as a primitive form of sexual stimulus, no doubt owing to the stinging influence of the nettles being effective without entailing much actual punishment. According to Bloch, Dr Johann Christoph Westphal was a firm believer in *urtication* as a remedy for sexual impotence.

An indication of the stimulatory powers of *urtication* is to be found in its application at one time to the treatment of disease. It was so employed not by quacks but by reputable medical practitioners. Dr Millingen, writing a century and a quarter ago, says:

"In a medical point of view, *urtication*, or stinging with nettles, is a practice not sufficiently appreciated. In many instances, especially in cases of paralysis, it is more efficacious than blistering or stimulating frictions. Its effects, although perhaps less permanent, are more general and diffused over the limb. This process has been found effectual in restoring heat to the lower extremities; and a case of obstinate lethargy was cured by Corvisart by repeated *urtication* of the whole body. During the action of the stimulus, the patient, who was a young man, would open his eyes and laugh, but sink again into profound sleep. His perfect cure, however, was obtained in three weeks."*

There is a significant admission by Festus, an early Roman writer, that there were men "who allowed themselves to be whipped for money". These whippers were referred to as *Flagratores*. Lucian refers also to a philosopher named Peregrinus who regularly whipped himself in public.

Many other references are to be found in ancient literature dealing with the connexion between whipping and sexual libido, and the consequent dangers of this and allied forms of punishment.

Vatsyayana, the author of the Hindu erotological manual known as the *Kama Sutra*,† refers to the effects of whipping upon libido; and a confirmatory statement appears in the *Talmud*. Later, the Abbé Boileau provides additional evidence.

It is significant that Hogarth's pictorial delineation of prostitution shows a rod of birch on the wall over the harlot's bed.

* J. G. Millingen, *Curiosities of Medical Experience*, second revised edition, London, 1839, p. 317.

† The *Kama Sutra* of Vatsyayana is available in this same Luxor Press series at 9s. 6d.

According to Petreus, in the olden days, in Germany, a whip was looked upon by the husband as an indispensable appurtenance to the bedroom.

In *The Presbyterian Lash or Noctroff's Maid Whipt*, a seventeenth-century satire on the then common practice of gentlemen whipping their maid-servants, there is a passage reading: "I warrant he thought that the tickling of the wench's buttocks with the rod would provoke her to lechery."

A remarkable case of school flogging is described in *A History of the Rod* by Cooper, and although this writer makes no direct or explicit connotation between whipping and sex, there can be little room for doubt that the incident had a purely sexual basis. Briefly told, the facts, according to Cooper's account, to which I am indebted, are these. In 1815, Lieutenant-General Sir Eyre Coote was charged before the Lord Mayor of London with "improper and indecent conduct". The charge was made by the officials of Christ's Hospital. After adjournment, the charge was ultimately dismissed. But rumour was busy, and in the end a further inquiry was held, which resulted in Sir Eyre Coote being dismissed from the service. It was alleged that this 'gallant gentleman' had visited the school and paid certain of the boys to allow themselves to be whipped by himself and also, in turn, to use the whip upon his own naked buttocks. Several boys, giving evidence, stated that they had been paid sums of eighteenpence and two shillings each, and the nurse affirmed that on entering the schoolroom unexpectedly she found "a gentleman uncovered as low as his knees from his breeches". She called the porter and gave "the gentleman" into custody.

There is little room for doubt that, from the beginning of civilisation, some knowledge of the effects of flagellation as a sexual stimulant has been pretty widespread in certain strata of society at least, and the paucity of references to whipping for erotic purposes is no indication that the practice was either comparatively unknown or rarely indulged in. What probably is nearer the truth is that erotic flagellation was a common practice in the libidinous aristocratic sections of society of each age and nation, but that the Church and State succeeded largely in preventing, or expunging from contemporary literature, any actual intimation of the more sexually stimulating characteristics of the practice.

It is therefore not to be wondered at that, as a result of these whispered references and surreptitious hints, fustigation gained for itself a reputation altogether at variance with the truth. It came to be looked upon as an efficient aphrodisiac in all circumstances and for all individuals; it was credited with producing greatly exaggerated and often ridiculous results; much as today various drugs are considered to possess most fantastic stimulatory powers.

As civilisation expanded, and complete suppression or censorship became difficult and, to a certain degree, impossible, surreptitious references to the practice of flagellation increased in number and degree, until, during the eighteenth and nineteenth centuries, there was no lack of references to the existence of the vice as a means of erotic stimulation. Judging from these accounts it would appear that the tendency (apart from such forms of erotic flagellation as were disguised under the name of religion) was for the practice to be largely restricted to brothels. Bloch, who has given a good deal of attention to the subject, affirms that "from the close of the eighteenth century and throughout the nineteenth century these brothels (special flagellation brothels) were a characteristic feature of London prostitution".* The list of these brothels is a formidable one. There was a particularly notorious establishment in Bedford Street, run by a Mrs Collet and visited by no less a personage than George IV. There was another famous establishment in Carlisle Street, Soho. There was a brothel run by Emma Richardson in Regent Street; another owned by Mrs Phillips in Upper Belgrave Place; yet another in Gilbert Street, where Mrs Shepherd reigned. And there were many more. All were profitable. Some of the more fashionable establishments netted fortunes for their owners. Possibly the most notorious, and certainly the most profitable of the lot, was Mrs Theresa

* Iwan Bloch, *Sex Life in England*, p. 218.

Berkley's place in Charlotte Street, which was the rendezvous for the wealthy voluptuaries of London in the early decades of the nineteenth century. Mrs Berkley earned the sobriquet of "queen of her profession" and invented the famous "Berkley Horse", a flagellating device which played a major part in the accumulation of her fortune. She died in 1836, leaving the very considerable sum (for those days) of £10,000.* Another notorious establishment in King's Road, Chelsea, run by a woman named Sarah Potter (*alias* Stewart), was raided by the police in July, 1863, and its proprietress arrested.† This prosecution resulted in many of the more blatant establishments having to close their doors, though undoubtedly 'flagellation brothels' continued to exist in secret.

Coming to recent times, it is well known that many of the Continental brothels catering for wealthy decadents, perverts and voluptuaries, were equipped with various types of whips and canes for the express purpose of stimulating or awakening sexual excitement, and although brothels as such have been officially abolished in virtually all European countries, prostitution and even establishments of various kinds still exist in a great many cities. A flagellation house only a short distance from the Rembrandtsplein in Amsterdam, for instance, which is still in being, is said to have been flourishing for something like a century.

Many London street-walkers, prior to 1959, had flagellating appliances in their rooms, and it was not unusual for them to mention this fact as an inducement when they were soliciting.‡ Frequently erotic flagellation flourishes under euphemised names. 'Massage' is sometimes nothing else but 'hand flagellation', for slapping with the hands has much the same effects

* Ironically enough, Mrs Berkley's executors after her death bequeathed this interesting apparatus to the Royal Society of Arts. See also *The Cruel and the Meek* (Luxor Press, 9s. 6d.), pp. 160 and 171.

† For much of this information relating to the "flagellation brothels" which flourished in London during the eighteenth and nineteenth centuries I am indebted to Dr Iwan Bloch's *Sex Life in England*, Panurge Press, New York, 1934.

‡ George Ryley Scott, *Ladies of Vice* (Luxor Press, 9s. 6d.).

155

as whipping or birching, and is frequently preferred. Kiernan asserted that it was common in America and that in advertisements concerning 'massage shops' in Chicago, it was by no means unusual for a subsidiary announcement to read "Flagellation a speciality".

It is, of course, manifestly impossible to ascertain with even the faintest hope of anything resembling accuracy the extent to which flagellation is practised. It is essentially a surreptitious affair, and its practitioners surround the whole thing with elaborate protective camouflage. Similarly, it is impossible to say in what country flagellation flourishes most extensively, and there seems little ground for Bloch's statement that "England is today the classic land of sexual flagellation". If the truth could be got at, it is probable that the practice exists in every civilised country. To a large extent it goes with prostitution, as in the main it is undoubtedly to prostitutes that impotent men and perverts suggest the employment of such a method of stimulating their waning or abnormal appetites; and it is similarly usually prostitutes who are willing either to wield the whip or, more rarely, to allow themselves to be whipped by sadists in return for money. Certainly, also, as the criminal records show, there are cases among girls outside the professional prostitute class, but they are not by any means so common.

It is customary for the general public to pay little attention to the veiled references they may see in the Press to cases of sexual flagellation, and to put them down as manifestations of some queer and abnormal impulse in human nature. Especially is this so today when flagellation has ceased altogether to be practised as a religious penance, and is rarely even resorted to as a form of punishment.

The idea of a man being whipped by a woman or even of a man whipping a woman, for any purpose at all, appears so abnormal, so strange, and so esoteric, as to be immediately set down in popular imagination as a form of insanity. This attempted explanation is, however, much too facile to be true. Insanity has rarely anything to do with the matter. Even the sadist is rarely insane. The assumption that the Marquis de Sade was insane, despite his incarceration in a lunatic asylum, is founded upon the most dubious evidence (see Chapter XVIII).

Medical, scientific and sociological writers have given the matter some attention; and, in the past, when ideas respecting sexual physiology and psychology were necessarily crude, many curious attempts were made to explain the phenomenon. Before tracing the true cause of such excitation as results from flagellation, it will be interesting to glance at these various hypotheses.

The most ancient of the scientists, then known as astrologers, glibly put down the cause of sexual flagellation to the stars. The influence of the stars was a fine panacea trotted out to explain everything which in those days was inexplicable or outside their comprehension. Picus, however, would have none of it. He criticised the hypothesis on the ground, and quite sanely, that if the stars were the cause of erotic flagellation, we should find the whole population submitting themselves to the stimulating influence of the whip. His own hypothesis, shared with Aristotle, Coelius and Galen, was that the practice was neither more nor less than a habit: a vice developed during youth, much in the way that the vice of masturbation was acquired and developed during youth. And this explanation seems to have sufficed, in so far as any explanation was sought or required, until well into the seventeenth century, when John Henry Meibomius, the physician to whose writings we have already had occasion to refer, set forth another hypothesis, which, although not accounting fully for the phenomenon, was more in accord with the truth than anything advanced before, and certainly approached to within measurable distance of the explanation advanced in accordance with modern scientific sexological research.

To understand the hypothesis advanced by Meibomius, it is necessary to glance for a moment at the position of sexual physiology at that time.

The art of medicine was in a very primitive stage of

development; of the glandular secretions little or nothing was known; physiological processes were only dimly understood; psychological influences were not known at all. The existence of spermatozoa and their function in the physiology of conception were yet to be discovered; the sources of the various constituents of the seminal fluid were unmapped.

The external sexual organs were looked upon purely as apparatuses connected with the act of coition itself, and as having nothing directly to do with the process of generation. The source of the seed which was responsible for the sex act resulting in the birth of a child, and which, it was thought, had a lot to do with the pleasure connected with the act, was supposed to be in the loins, synonymously referred to as the reins or the sides. Coincidentally, all these terms were used as synonyms for the organ of generation itself, for venereal passion, for lust, and for concupiscence generally. Thus, in the Bible, we read:

"Yea, my reins shall rejoice when thy lips speak right things." (Proverbs xxiii. 16.)

And again:

"And I will kill her children with death; and all the churches shall know that I am he that searcheth the reins and hearts: and I will give unto every one of you according to your works." (Revelation ii. 23.)

Saint Augustine affirms that the word reins signifies the pleasure of venery. Petronius, Tertullian, Catullus, Martial, Ovid, Hesychius, Junius, Apuleius, Nicolas Lyra, Suetonius and others, all make similar connotations. Indeed, Juvenal's lines summarise the prevailing opinion of the day:

> When music and when wine to lust conspire,
> Provoke the blood, and set the loins on fire.

This view, therefore, that the kidneys and adjacent parts were the seat of generative power and sexual capacity, was coincident with the opinion that anything which tended to increase the temperature of these parts similarly increased sexual passion, and analogously, anything which reduced the temperature caused a corresponding diminution in sexual passion. These ideas, which were undoubtedly solidified by, and may have had their origin in, the observed 'heat' of animals during the rutting season, induced the elaboration of various curious remedies for excessive venery. Meibomius instances several of these remedies. That of Pliny deserves special mention. For the diminution of an appetite for venery he advocated the wearing of lead plates on the loins, citing, in support of his prescription, the case of one Calvas, an orator, who, although of so libidinous a nature that the mere sight of a female sufficed to provoke an emission, was cured of the distressing malaise by wearing these plates of lead. Various other contemporary medical authorities held similar views, and adopted variations of Pliny's method of reducing the temperature of the kidneys, liver and adjacent parts, as a remedy for excessive sexual appetite. Thus Galen used similar metal plates as a cure for night emissions in athletes, and as a means of diminishing sexual passion wherever continence was advisable; he prescribed cold-water bandages in cases of priapism; Aetius and Oribasius pointed out that lying on the back tended to cause overheating of the loins;* Coelius advocated the application of sponges saturated in cold water as a sure specific for cooling the fever of lust. These were truly heroic measures, and one can well believe in their temporary efficiency—I can hardly imagine any man, however susceptible to female charms, being in a state for love-making when wearing a pair of clumsy metal plates clamped round his body, or even when incommoded by a cold-water bandage.

The opposite contention, that warmth assisted and promoted venereal appetite, was a common belief for many hundreds of years, and on this basis were recommended many

* A belief that lying on the back increased lust and was the cause of various afflictions pervaded ancient literature. Aristotle considered it to be the cause of venereal disease, and inferred that animals were free from this affliction because they did not lie on their backs.

of the aphrodisiacs which are to be found besprinkling ancient erotic literature.

Meibomius sums up the whole position thus:

"From all of which I draw this consequence, that the loins in general, and the parts they consist of, contribute chiefly to venery, and principally their veins and arteries; but that the grand instrument of all this is the parenchyma of the reins, by which the seed first begins to be elaborated, and that it is perfected and acquires an equable consistence in its descent through the other seminal vessels."*

This seventeenth-century physician and scientist then proceeds to elaborate his hypothesis to account for the success of flagellation, either with whips or other instruments, in exciting sexual passion. Fustigation warms and inflames the kidneys and adjacent parts and promotes the flow of semen, and further the pain inseparable from such punishment stimulates the organs of generation to an extent beyond their normal powers.

It is here that Meibomius, in the midst of his fanciful and pseudo-scientific explanations and arguments, hits upon a part of the truth. He gets at the right result by the wrong means: a phenomenon that has always been common enough, and which is common enough today.

We have already seen that of all factors capable of arousing emotion, pain, provided always it does not reach a degree of intensity where it ranks as torture, is the most powerful; that pain, by increasing the secretory powers of the adrenal glands and reinvigorating tired or enfeebled muscles and nerves, stimulates the individual to the achievement of temporary efforts far beyond his normal capacity.† Now, it is an established fact that the region of the gluteus (that is, the buttocks and base of the spine) is supplied with nerves corresponding to, and intimately connected with, the nerves governing the sexual function. We have seen that ancient physicians were

* John Henry Meibomius, *A Treatise on the Use of Flogging in Medicine and Venery* (originally published in Latin in 1645).

† See Chapter II.

aware of the effect which pain in the buttocks and neighbourings parts had on the sexual libido; the similar effects of applications to the lumbar region of hot poultices or caustic plasters; in short, the sexual stimulatory properties of anything destined to increase the engorging of the genital passages, and particularly of the penis, with blood. Congestion due to these causes, or to the effects of chemical aphrodisiacs, is capable of inducing erections. It is because of this that flagellation is bound to have some effect in the relief of any form of impotence which is neither permanent nor congenital. Even friction of the skin in the genital regions will stimulate sexual excitement; hence the popularity of massage, and especially of massage following immediately upon a hot bath. After all, masturbation is merely friction or irritation of the genitals.

There is, therefore, invariably a danger that whipping, whatever may be its basic object, and wherever it is not of such a degree of severity as to rank as torture or heavy punishment, will induce sexual stimulation. In children and adolescents there is a risk of *any form* of castigation on the buttocks or anal region stirring up sexual activity. In this connexion Vecki says:

"Flogging on the bare back or buttocks is apt to incite to premature activity the sexual organs, or, rather, the nerves which lead from the centre of erection through the spinal cord ... such blows applied on the back and buttocks constitute a brutally empiric aphrodisiac."*

In a strikingly analogous way, psychological sexual excitation induced through thoughts of one's lover, through the sight of a pretty girl, through fetishistic aphrodisiacs, through pornographic pictures or reading erotic literature, arouse corresponding excitation in the sexual regions; and peripheral sexual excitation, such as masturbation, kissing, contact with women, similarly arouse psychological sexual sensations. As a rule, it requires the existence of one predisposing condition

* Victor G. Vecki, *Sexual Impotence*, fifth edition, Saunders, Philadelphia, 1915.

only to arouse or excite all the other analogous, corresponding or related conditions.

The evils connected with flogging and birching, to which I have alluded in this chapter, are all the more serious because they are so very often overlooked or ignored. Moreover, these evils are such as are *likely* to occur whenever and wherever corporal punishment is employed as a punitive measure.

It is significant and important that the likelihood of corporal punishment arousing, exciting or developing erotic feelings is particularly marked where children and adolescents are concerned. Only too often did a whipping, ordered unthinkingly, in the mistaken notion that it might scare the boy into the straight and narrow path, merely succeed in turning a normal individual into a sexual decadent or a pervert. So true is this, and so great is the risk, that it might safely be said that the birching of a child, whether in the school, the home, or the prison, was inevitably and invariably, from a sexual point of view, potentially dangerous.

There are, too, as we shall see later, cases where, in youngsters, some *latent* form of masochism or sadism is present, only waiting for circumstances to arise which will turn the budding tendency into an active vice. In any such case flogging would provide just such an arousing and developing agent. The case of Jean-Jacques Rousseau is as instructive as it is notable. (See Chapter XVIII.)

Finally, there is to be considered the effect of whipping upon the person wielding the instrument of flagellation. Here, we are confronted with the risk, as grave as it is inevitable, of the development of sadism, even in cases where no tendency actually exists already; while, in all cases of active sadism, there is the 'lust' for cruelty manifesting itself in brutal and cunning extensions of the punishment that has been prescribed.

All these matters we shall consider in detail in the next chapter.

XVIII: PATHOLOGICAL ASPECTS OF CORPORAL
PUNISHMENT

THERE are many misconceptions connected with sadism. The term itself has been so loosely used in recent years that where any knowledge, however superficial, of the thing exists, popular imagination is likely to give to it something quite outside and irrelevant to its true meaning; the more so as journalists and even scientific writers often use the term sadism as a synonym for unvarnished cruelty. It is a usage, and a growing usage, which is likely to cause much misunderstanding. Sadism involves much more than mere cruelty. And coincidentally it never involves cruelty purely for cruelty's sake. Although the sadist is always, consciously or unconsciously, cruel either in deed or thought, cruelty *per se* does not imply sadism. Thus, there are thousands of cruel persons in the world who are not sadists; just as there are individuals who, apart from certain specific sadistic acts which give them pleasure, abhor cruelty. Indeed, the infliction of pain unconnected with any thought of conscious cruelty is the aim of the sadist; and coincidentally, it is precisely this which distinguishes him from the ordinary member of society whose cruelty has no sexual connotations.

Sadism consists in sexual pleasure or sensation induced through the infliction of pain, suffering, or humiliation, in another person or an animal. It also includes sexual pleasure induced by the sight of suffering inflicted upon another person or an animal by a third party. Again, it includes sexual pleasure induced by reading, or thinking about suffering or pain or humiliation: a form of the perversity which may be described as vicarious or symbolic sadism.

In its most primitive and basic form it exists, as we have seen, in the love-bite which is so often associated with the sex act. Here we see the dissonance, already mentioned, which undoubtedly exists between cruelty and pain. In the love-bite there is no notion of being cruel, there is no conscious association with cruelty. And, further, whichever of the partners is bitten, if in the throes of sexual ecstasy, he or she experiences no pain. What in any other circumstances would prove painful, is submerged in and actually a means of intensifying sexual enjoyment.

A realisation of these facts will help to interpret the seeming inconsequence and abnormality of the sadist's conduct, which is merely an extension or development of this primitive and fundamental love-bite. The sadist, whether his aberration manifests itself in active flagellation or in any one of a score of other forms, gets his sexual thrill from the pain he is giving or witnessing or imagining. The feelings and the reactions of his victim are entirely consequent upon individual sexual idiosyncrasies. For the most part these victims feel no sexual connotations, and therefore they experience pain and degradation only; as in the case of prisoners in jails and the recalcitrant schoolboys who were so extensively whipped in past ages. It is only the masochist who experiences sexual pleasure in submission to what, in all other circumstances, would constitute pain.

Undoubtedly sadism is, in some cases, a good deal mixed up with the will-to-power, to which I have already made some reference (see Chapter I). The one does not necessarily imply the other; but often they are co-existent. There is nothing in the world which is better calculated than is a cruel act to express, in easily and fully understandable terms, the power of one individual over another. The analogousness of the coital act with an act of cruelty may not at first sight be apparent, but it exists nevertheless. In certain individuals copulation represents, supremely, the *subjection of the woman to the man.*

The truth of this will be manifest if one reflects that the man who succeeds in securing the surrender of a woman outside marriage generally looks down on her. He considers her in the light of a conquest. He considers her as an inferior being. Even in marriage itself there is very often this same feeling of having subjected another individual to the will of the master.

There can be no question that, in certain cases, an act of cruelty can completely take the place of coition. The man, thwarted in his plans to effect the sexual surrender of the woman may, in his lust for power, force her to surrender, or he may subject her to some cruel or humiliating act with or without attendant rape. The helplessness and the subjection of the victim serve to inflame his ego.

Where we get the will-to-power functioning coincidentally in the forms of both sexual passion and cruelty, we have true sadism. And as both are so intimately associated, and provide such strong analogues, it is easy to see how the one *breeds* the other. The arousing of sexual excitation induces cruelty, as many a woman, even before her honeymoon has come to an inglorious end, has found out to her cost. The perpetration of a cruel act induces lust, as many a victim has discovered, often to the accompaniment of dismay and consternation.

In some form or other it may safely be assumed that these twin emotive states of lust and cruelty are existent in a very large proportion of men, and a very much smaller number of women. These cases may be looked upon as representing incipient forms of sadism. It only requires an upsetting, as it were, temporary or otherwise, of the normal processes, a psychological storm, resulting in psychosis, such as happens often enough, and the normal individual may be transformed into a sexual monster who throws aside all the inhibitions imposed by society, and functions as one of those perverts who from time to time provide sensational copy for the daily Press.

The notion that sadism is a comparatively modern pheno-menon is a fallacy. It is older than civilisation. Only, in early days, it was probably not recognised as a sexual aberration: it ranked as ordinary cruelty. Nero was a sadist. So was Tiberius. So was Caligula. So was Domitian. So was Heliogabalus. So were a hundred other historical personages.

It was Krafft-Ebing who gave to those aberrations where sexual pleasure is secured from the infliction or witnessing of punishment and pain, the name of sadism. He was led to employ this term through the fact that the notorious Marquis de Sade had been the first man to make a thorough and comprehensive study of this particular phenomenon. Indeed this de Sade has had so great an influence, and let in so much light upon this specific form of sexual perversity, that it will be well to glance briefly at the man and his writings before proceeding further in our examination.

Born in 1740, Donatien-Alphonse-François, Marquis de Sade, a man of distinguished parentage and great culture, was a product of that period in French history preceding the Revolution when libidinism, voluptuousness and debauchery reached degrees of intensity and universality rivalling those of the worst days of Ancient Rome as described by Petronius. To form any estimate at all of the crimes attributed to de Sade it is essential to bear all this in mind. At that time civilised society, throughout Europe, delighted in practising and witnessing acts of cruelty. Bull-baiting was a favourite sport of the English aristocracy. Paris wallowed in every form of sexual perversity.

It was in such a setting, then, that was staged *L'Affaire Keller*, the sadistic act for which de Sade was first sent to prison, and which, with a subsequent crime and his notorious writings, were to brand him as the most fiendish sexual pervert of all time. The incident happened in Paris on April 3, 1768. De Sade was accosted by the pretty Rose Keller, a young widow in humble and penurious circumstances, who asked him for help. He took her to his *petite maison* to spend the night; and, according to the girl's subsequent statement, after forcing her to remove every stitch of clothing, whipped her severely and indecently, dressed the weals made by the whip, and left her locked in the room. The following day de Sade returned, inflicted several small wounds on her body with a knife, anointed them with more of the healing balm* he had used the previous day, and again left her behind lock and bar. Rose managed to make her escape through the window, however, and went to the police with her story, and her scarred body as evidence of its truth. The upshot of the affair was a short term of imprisonment for de Sade, and an indemnity for Rose Keller.

Four years later de Sade again figured in a sensational criminal case. While in Marseilles he visited a brothel and treated the girls to a sort of banquet. When the feasting was at its height he brought out a box of chocolates, which, as it afterwards transpired, contained cantharides, an aphrodisiac which enjoyed a great vogue at the time. Apparently most of those present, as a result of eating the sweetmeats, suffered from a mild form of poisoning, though there would appear to be no evidence for Bauchment's statement that two prostitutes died. At any rate de Sade had to leave the country in order to avoid arrest. On his return to France some years later, on this and other charges, real or apocryphal, he was arrested and sent to prison, and in prison he remained for fourteen years, from 1777 to 1790. It was during this prolonged period of imprisonment that de Sade wrote the most notorious of the pornographic novels which created such a sensation, and which have largely sufficed to cause the very name de Sade to be linked up with the vilest forms of sexual perversity.

The most famous and the best known of de Sade's works is undoubtedly *Justine*, the story of a girl whose ambition is to lead a life of virtue and goodness, but who comes up against everything that is vile, degrading, vicious and perverse. In this story of Justine's adventures, de Sade manages to catalogue and describe very nearly every conceivable sexual crime. *Juliette*, a companion volume, written some few years later, chronicles the life of Justine's sister. The girl Juliette is the

* The woman herself, in her accusatory deposition, alleged that de Sade poured red and white wax on her wounds. For a fuller account of the case and for further information concerning de Sade, see *The Cruel and the Meek*, by Dr Walter Braun (Luxor Press, 9s. 6d.).

exact opposite of Justine: she is a vicious, self-seeking, unscrupulous gold-digger, who wallows in every form of sexual depravity and finally emerges successful and prosperous.

Actually de Sade does not excel as a novelist. Both *Justine* and *Juliette* bristle with defects. They are incredibly and almost insufferably long; their author stumbles and staggers into almost every morass that a novelist could possibly find; the stories themselves are broken-backed. Were it not for their rank pornography, I doubt if they would have outlived de Sade's life. His one volume of short stories, *Les Crimes de l'Amour*, from the point of view of the writer's art, is even worse than his novels.

But they were successes, these books. They went into edition after edition. They were sold in the Parisian bookshops, and they were not, at the time of their publication, deemed to be obscene; which, considering the morals of the day, is no matter for surprise. In view of this it may seem strange that de Sade should have been confined to prison and asylum for twenty-seven years of his life. The popular idea that his incarceration was due entirely to his sexual escapades and pornographic writings is an erroneous one. True enough, this was the ostensible reason given to the world, but it was not the real reason.

De Sade, altogether apart from his writings on sex, showed himself as a fearless and an incisive critic of the Bible and of Christianity.* He made an enemy of the Church, which in turn assailed him with all its venom and spleen. In addition, he published a political satire which aroused the wrath and enmity of Napoleon, then at the height of his fame and power. A fatal move, this. It was at Napoleon's instigation that proceedings were started against de Sade in 1801, that he was once again imprisoned, that his books were burned; that, finally, he was certified, quite unjustly, as a lunatic, and clapped into a prison asylum for the rest of his life. It was a favourite

* His *Dialogue between a Priest and a Dying Man* is a masterpiece of religious criticism, and, from a literary point of view, far in advance of his novels.

trick of the Corsican despot's, this confinement of his enemies in asylums. The Abbé Fournier, de Laage, Désorgues, were other such victims.

De Sade was indubitably addicted to the vice which is now decorated with his name; he found sexual pleasure in the infliction of pain, and even more in the contemplation of it. Also there seems little doubt that he practised homosexual vice. But there is no evidence that he was the sexual monster that legend asserts; there is no evidence that he ever came within measurable distance of equalling the debaucheries of the Caesars, or of Gilles de Rais, or of many another sadist who has graced the pages of history. It is to his writings more than to any overt sexual acts that is ascribable the reputation which he earned for himself. There are grounds for thinking that, in his later years, de Sade derived his sexual satisfaction mainly from imagining sadistic acts—vicarious sadism is possibly a far more widely spread form of the perversion than active sadism.

And yet sadistic acts are common enough. The sight of blood, in certain circumstances, awakens passion, as in the numerous instances of lust-murder. Such a case was that of the notorious Jack the Ripper, the anonymous perpetrator of a series of sadistic murders which terrorised London some eighty years ago. The victims were all women, and their bodies were ripped open and mutilated in a most gruesome fashion. Occasionally, this species of lust takes eccentric forms, such as violating animals, or birds, and sometimes human cadavers. The case of the monomaniacal necrophile, Sergeant Bertrand, is a notorious and well authenticated example. According to his own statement in court, Bertrand began his revolting activities by securing corpses of various animals, which he mutilated to the accompaniment of the most intense pleasure. In time, animals ceased to satisfy, and he started visiting graveyards in the dead of night, disinterring recently buried bodies and mutilating them. In all, he succeeded in taking up fifteen corpses before his activities were discovered. His procedure was to dig up the cadavers with the aid of any implement he could secure and often with his bare hands, dissect the bodies with a knife or sword, and remove the entrails. He described his condition during this hideous task as one of extraordinary ecstasy.

Charles, King of Navarre, sometimes called, and with good reason, Charles the Bad, ironically enough furnished sadistic pleasure for thousands of spectators. He was burned to death in 1387 for sadistic and other crimes of the most repulsive description. Dimitri, son of Ivan the Cruel, deserved a similar fate—he had animals and birds killed slowly, feasting his eyes on the sight and gloating over the death struggles of his victims.

Marshal Gilles de Rais was executed in 1440 for the mutilation and murder of some eight hundred children. More recently, Krafft-Ebing records the case of Vacher the Ripper, who, in 1897, was tried and sentenced to death for the murder of a seventeen-year-old shepherd-boy named Portalier, and for several sadistic crimes to the commission of which he confessed. The list, according to Krafft-Ebing, was as lengthy as it was terrible. Vacher, who led the life of a tramp, began his vile career in March of 1894 by strangling a girl named Delhomme. In November of the same year he perpetrated a very similar crime, and again in the May of 1895. August of the same year found him committing two more murders, one victim being a girl of sixteen and the other a woman of fifty-eight years. The month following, he turned his attention to his own sex, killing a boy of fifteen named Palet. Five more victims were added to this formidable array before his arrest put a stop to these sanguinary and revolting atrocities.

Occasionally the sadistic impulse assumes bizarre forms which at first sight seem strangely unrelated to the lust for the infliction of pain. It may show itself in certain forms of pure destructiveness. The important excitatory influence which the colour red assumes in sexual stimulation partially accounts for the marked effects on all witnesses of flagellation as well as on active flagellants themselves. This lust-excitatory effect induced by the sight of the blood-reddened flesh is, according to Stekel, stressed by Bloch, who traces the cause of outbreaks of pyromania, in certain cases, to the search for a sadistic substitute for orthodox sexual gratification. Stekel gives instances, abstracted by Dr Missriegler from de Sade's writings, of pyromania manifesting itself in sadistic acts. There is the notable incident where the hospitals of Rome are deliberately set on fire. "Twenty thousand inmates perish during the eight days when the thirty-seven institutions burn down, while Olympia and Juliette attain great sexual acme at the sight of the conflagration."*

Sadism which manifests itself in the witnessing of suffering and pain has always found many opportunities for indulgence, and for this reason, next to mental pictures induced through the medium of written or pictorial descriptions, is probably by far the most popular and widespread form of sadism. A sadistic scene is featured in the mind, and it may have all the seeming reality of a hallucination. There must, however, be present in the individual some latent predisposition to the evocation of sexual emotion at, and its association with, the sight of pain, suffering, humiliation or cruelty.

History bristles with instances of kings and emperors enjoying the spectacle of certain of their subjects being killed or tortured. As we have seen, the annals of religion provide innumerable instances of sacrificial feasts, punishments, atonements, etc., which, stripped of their hypocritical trimmings, were, in many cases, purely sadistic practices flourishing under other names. Nero, Tiberius, Heliogabalus, Caracalla, Maxentius and others of the Romans gleefully watched the slaughtering of girls and boys; the Inquisitors showed no pity at the horrible death struggles of their victims; the Spanish nobility viewed with equal ecstasy the deaths of either the bull-fighters or their opponents; the English aristocracy feasted their eyes upon the dying struggles of fighting-cocks, bulls, bears and dogs.

In the days when executions were performed publicly, sadists revelled in the spectacle. The public turned out in their thousands to witness the torture of the unhappy victim in the

* Wilhelm Stekel, *Peculiarities of Behaviour*, Williams & Norgate, 1925, p. 140.

days when those condemned to death were burned at the stake or broken on the wheel. When the rope, or the axe, or the guillotine, took the place of the older and more barbaric methods, public excitement in the witnessing of an execution abated little. Even those who were not sadists in any real sense, evidently had a taste for cruelty wellnigh unbelievable. Writers have, in the past, commented freely on these exhibitions of mass cruelty, and the accounts make sorry reading. When Damiens, who attempted to kill Louis XV of France, was executed in the January of 1757, according to the account of Casanova, who was himself present, every available spot overlooking the place of execution was packed with gloating, gibbering, enthusiastic men and women, who revelled in the sight of the doomed man's terrible torture and the prolonged agony which preceded his death.* Goncourt tells of an Englishman hiring a room overlooking the scaffold on which an execution by hanging was to take place: knowing the excitatory effects of such an affair, he intended bringing with him a young lady who, presumably, was not proving an easy conquest.

So long as executions in public were allowed in England, these sordid, sadistic performances were apparently looked upon by the majority of the spectators as entertainments on a par with the modern boxing contest or football match. From far and near the public in their thousands flocked to the places of execution, the wealthy paying high prices for positions ensuring a particularly intimate view of the execution. Indeed, many wealthy sadists made a practice of witnessing every execution possible. One such was Horace Walpole's close friend, George Selwyn, of whom it was said that his greatest pleasure in life was to see a man put to death. Another noted character who took pleasure in witnessing the death throes of criminals was Samuel Johnson's biographer, Boswell. He rarely missed an execution at Newgate.

It is a noteworthy point, which has been remarked upon again and again by contemporary historians, that in those days

* A fuller reference to the execution of Damiens appears in *The Cruel and the Meek* (Luxor Press, 9s. 6d.), p. 83.

when social distinctions were in all circumstances of normalcy most sharply defined and clearly drawn, at these spectacles of torture and cruelty such distinctions were, for the moment, totally forgotten. Peers and peasants mixed with each other on terms of equality; they exchanged jests and jokes with the greatest of good humour. This, more perhaps than anything else, indicates how great an effect on the emotions had these inhuman, revolting and barbaric spectacles.

And the women were as excited as the men. The assumption, often made, that sadism in all its forms is exclusively a male perversion, is a fallacy. The study of sexual psychology disproves this. And history provides evidence of sadistic qualities in women in all abundance. Messalina delighted in witnessing the suffering of human beings of both sexes, as well as in wielding the whip with her own capable hands; Catherine de'Medici confessed to experiencing the keenest satisfaction and emotion in seeing ladies of the court stripped to the buff and flagellated in her presence. More and worse, she was as pronouncedly sadistic as were many of those Roman emperors who flourished centuries before her time. She was mainly responsible for the terrible massacre of Saint Bartholomew, experiencing a degree of ecstasy which she herself described as like "bathing in roses", at the horrible sight.

Of considerable interest is the case of Edith Cadivec, recorded by Wulffen.* This Cadivec woman ran an exclusive school of languages in Vienna, her pupils being drawn from the wealthiest classes. She posed, too, as a philanthropic educator, her advertisements stating that she was prepared to give lessons to poorer children without charge, and even to adopt a few pupils. The reason for this apparent magnanimity was revealed at the sensational trial of 1924, which followed in the wake of certain complaints. It appeared that the 'school of languages' was a flagellating parlour. The 'students' were perverts and debauchees. Men and women in the highest walks in life, and holding important appointments and positions, were regular

* Erich Wulffen, *Woman as a Sexual Criminal*, American Ethnological Press, New York, 1934.

visitors to the Cadivec apartment. The children she 'adopted' were whipped for the sadistic gratification of the students and visitors. According to her own confession, Cadivec felt a degree of pleasure, when punishing children, which reached great heights of intensity. She was sentenced to imprisonment for six years, which sentence was subsequently shortened to four years.

The sadistic pleasure secured by pedagogues from the whipping of children was by no means rare in the days when flogging was part of the educational system of most European countries. Udall, for ten years head-master of Eton College, and notorious for his habit of flogging boys on the slightest of pretexts, often on grounds that were palpably invented, subsequently confessed to securing pleasure in this way, and to the commission of overt sexual acts.

In many cases the avowed disciplinary value of flagellation in schools and colleges was a mere pretence to enable sadists to secure sexual titillation. So true was this in England at one time that in Continental countries the statement in an educational prospectus and in advertisements that 'English methods' were employed was an indication in certain circles that the 'school' was in reality a brothel where sexual perversions were practised.

A special form of sadism is known as 'pricking'. Its practitioners secure pleasure through 'stabbing', 'pricking', or 'cutting' women and children in various parts of the body. The injuries are usually slight and may be effected on buses, trams, in theatres, and in all places where crowds congregate. Féré gives a case of a sadist of this type arrested in Paris for cutting the ears of women.*

In some cases, through fear of consequences, the sadist leaves human beings alone and transfers his energies to animals and birds. Instances are by no means rare. There have been, from time to time, outcrops of maiming and killing cattle, horses, sheep and dogs in certain districts, while large numbers of isolated instances never get into the newspapers.

* Ch. Féré, *The Sexual Instinct: Its Evolution and Dissolution*, London, 1900, p. 150.

Possibly the most widespread form of sadism, especially today, as I have already mentioned, is the finding of sexual pleasure and excitation in literary descriptions and pictorial representations of sadistic scenes provided by books, films and plays. Sadism of this type is related to the dreaming of similar scenes, and the imagining of vivid pictures of flagellatory and other acts which reach such degrees of realism as to rank as almost equivalent to those of a definitely hallucinatory nature. Féré terms this form "imaginary sadism", and says "it is hardly ever observed except in neuropaths".* Krafft-Ebing classifies such cases as belonging to "ideal sadism", and instances the case of a twenty-two-year-old man who obtained pleasure from inventing stories of flagellating orgies, drawing pictures of similar scenes, and so on.

For the most part, symbolic forms of sadism begin and end in the imagination. The harm is of a cumulative nature, and lies in the psychological effects on the individual addicted to this particular form of perversion. There may be, and no doubt are, odd cases where the symbolic form constitutes the first step on the path to active sadism. Gilles de Rais attributed his overt sadistic acts to his youthful readings of the accounts by Suetonius of the orgies of torture and murder in which Tiberius, Caracalla and others wallowed. In this there was probably some modicum of truth. Imagination can fill in many blanks, a fact which quacks, mountebanks, theologians, politicians, and others, have been quick to take advantage of throughout the ages.

The objection to sadism, an objection which cannot but be felt by any humanitarian, is precisely of the same brand as the objection to cruelty in any one of its manifold forms. The one is as much to be decried as the other. The only difference between sadism and any other form of cruelty is in the admixture of sexual pleasure or satisfaction. Hunting in all its forms, pigeon-shooting, butchering, cock-fighting, which may or may not be combined with sadism, are hardly less objectionable, and as strongly to be deplored and denounced.

* Ch. Féré, *The Sexual Instinct: Its Evolution and Dissolution*, London, 1900, p. 149.

Masochism is the desire for punishment, subjection or humiliation at the hands of the opposite sex, and, in rare cases, in relation to the same sex.

It is far more widely practised than sadism. There are many reasons for its greater prevalence. In the first place it is far easier for the active masochist to put into practice his perversity than it is for the active sadist. Obviously so. There is never any great difficulty in finding someone who will be willing to inflict punishment or degradation; there is often great difficulty in finding those who will submit to punishment even if one is willing to pay them to adopt the role. Also, while the sadist may be prepared to go to any lengths, even to the extent of maiming or killing his victim, in the case of the masochist this rarely, if ever, happens, the instinct of self-preservation acting as an efficient preventive.*

The phenomenon of masochism *per se* is nothing new. Like sadism it is as old as civilisation. It is the term masochism which is of comparatively recent vintage, being derived from the name Sacher-Masoch, the writer who was responsible for the clearest, most poetical and most salacious description of the perversity that exists in all literature.

From Schlichtegroll's biography of the novelist, from his own writings, and from his first wife's autobiography, there seems little doubt that the environmental conditions under which his early and most susceptible years were passed had a good deal to do with the development of the perversion which was to affect so powerfully his later life. Cruelty, callousness and even bloodshed, were everyday affairs during Sacher-Masoch's adolescence; and the youngster had a taste of the heartless and sanguinary persecutions which marked the progress of the Polish revolution. It would appear that much of his perversion was of the imaginative type, that in a world of fantasy he liked to picture himself being threatened, humiliated and beaten by an imperious, domineering woman of great

* This point, as well as other points of contrast, is well brought out by Dr Walter Braun in *The Cruel and the Meek* (Luxor Press. 9s. 6d.), pp. 113-16.

personal charm, culture and beauty. In his novel, *Venus in Furs*,* his personal reaction to such domination is painted with meticulous accuracy, Severin, the main male character of the novel, who becomes the slave of the regal, arrogant Wanda, being a representation of himself. Says Severin, in a notable passage:

"The more easily a woman gives herself, the more quickly the man grows cold and arrogant. The more she is cruel and unfaithful to him, the more she ill-treats him, the more she plays with him, the less pity she shows him, the more she excites his desires, the more he loves her, the more he seeks her out. It has been so in all ages, since Helen of Troy and Delilah up to the two Catherines and Lola Montez."

Leopold von Sacher-Masoch married a young glove-maker of Graz, Aurora Rümelin, with whom he had previously had an *affaire* which culminated in the birth of a child. Aurora adopted the name of his heroine (Wanda) in *Venus in Furs*. She fulfilled the role of the imperious and majestic but lovely and fascinating tyrant of his dreams. Such a role was not an easy one to live up to. There was much disagreement. Eventually there was a separation and later a divorce. Subsequently the novelist married his secretary, Hulda Meister, and settled down, surprisingly enough, to the innocent and eminently respectable life of a country squire and rural benefactor. He died in 1895, at the age of fifty-nine.

There is a widespread idea, to which much weight is given by the statements of several writers on perversions, that masochism is peculiarly a feminine phenomenon and, correspondingly, that sadism is an exclusively masculine one. Some authorities go so far as to assert that masochism is, to a certain degree, a *natural* feminine characteristic, basing their argument upon the subjective state of woman in comparison with the possessive rights of man. The first contention is

* Published in this series by Luxor Press at 9s. 6d. For a much fuller account of Leopold von Sacher-Masoch see Dr Walter Braun, *The Cruel and the Meek* (Luxor Press, 9s. 6d.).

certainly an erroneous one; the second I believe to be greatly exaggerated, as masochism *per se* is no more *natural* to the female of the species than it is to the male. It is, I contend, purely a product of social, moral, and, in some cases, pathological conditions and circumstances, and it is, owing to these conditions and circumstances, mainly, in the present social and economic dispensation, a male characteristic.

If the truth could be got at I fully believe it would be found that the male masochists are to the female as nine to one. It is a peculiarity of the average male that he is willing to subject himself, and secures pleasure from this subjection, to the autonomy of a beautiful woman. The dominance of the female is, however, a dominance of charm, of voluptuousness, of elegance, of beauty, or, in modern jargon, the dominance of sex-appeal. It is not the dominance of masculinity parading under a feminine skin and decorated with feminine trapperies.

There can be little question that Sacher-Masoch looked upon the perversity he described so elaborately as peculiarly a male phenomenon. In all his writings, the slavery of man to beautiful and lascivious women was constantly reiterated; and, according to Krafft-Ebing, at the head of a letter which Sacher-Masoch wrote to a correspondent in 1888, was "the picture of a luxuriant woman, with imperial bearing, only half covered with furs, and holding a riding-whip as if ready to strike",* this being in accordance with his concept of man having an almost universal "passion to play the slave". The same authority gives numerous cases, culled from the novelist's writings, of submission to the domination of women.

One of the reasons why so many people look upon masochism as so much more unlikely and so much more pathological than sadism, is the difficulty experienced in grasping the idea that anyone, in a normal condition, will *willingly* submit to punishment. It is easy to imagine the sadist inflicting punishment— there are too many cases of cruelty of all kinds to dispute its occurrence—but masochism is entirely another matter. It is

* Krafft-Ebing, *Psychopathia Sexualis*, p. 189.

important to remember, however, that pain is largely subjective —in the stress of a great emotion it disappears; in the stress of sexual emotion it may be transformed into pleasure. In the case of the masochist it *is* transformed into sexual ecstasy. In many cases of religious flagellation undoubtedly no pain was felt by the victim. Undoubtedly, too, much of the religious flagellation, and particularly self-flagellation, was distinctly masochistic in origin, the penitent or the martyr subjecting himself not to the majestic tyranny of a woman but to the omnipotence of God.

Masochistic phenomena sometimes take the shape of humiliations quite unconnected with cruelty. Practices like koprolagnia, urolagnia, and other degrading predilections, are frequent modes of expression, and these may or may not be connected, in addition, with fetishism.* In the days when religious fanaticism took obscure and abnormal forms scatological practices were common. Ezekiel, we are told, ate human excrement. Krafft-Ebing mentions, as significant, that Marie Alacoque "licked up" the excrement and sucked the festering sores of sick persons in order to 'mortify' herself; Antoinette Bouvignon de la Porte mixed faeces with her food.† These, like the commoner manifestations of self-mutilation, asceticism, martyrdom in all its forms, and self-denial, were decidedly masochistic in their origin, being rarely completely divorced from some (conscious or unconscious) sexual corollaries.

In its more remote aspects, masochism is sometimes the responsible factor in curious anomalies of human nature which would probably be difficult to explain as being due to any other basic cause or which could not be interpreted in any other way.

---

* In many savage races, in early Christianity, and in Mohammedanism, urine and faeces were both supposed to be charged with magical power. There are strong grounds for the assumption that the *original* Holy Water consisted of human urine. With the development of civilisation, urine lost many of its masochistic and fetishistic connotations. At one time it was used extensively by medical practitioners in England as a specific for many ailments.

† Krafft-Ebing, *Psychopathia Sexualis*, p. 186.

Thus, according to Stekel, the root cause of kleptomania is sometimes masochism. He says:

"Kleptomania bears certain relations to masochism. That is the reason why certain parapathiacs confess thefts and even murders of which they are not guilty, an occurrence that would otherwise remain unintelligible. These individuals are impelled to act thus by the desire to suffer punishment. Everybody knows that certain unruly children provoke punishments because such experiences are a source of pleasure to them. Paternal anger sometimes acts as a sexual stimulant in children."*

Actually, symbolic masochism is probably the most common form which the perversion takes. Here there is no actual whipping or other form of punishment, no practical or public humiliation. On the contrary, the masochist gets his thrill from imagining acts of perversion, from reading accounts of them, from feasting his eyes upon pictorial representations. Krafft-Ebing gives some remarkable instances. In one case, the subject was a man of twenty-six years, troubled with a masochistic desire to be "absolutely subject to the will and whims" of a mistress who would cause him to perform the most humiliating and disgusting tasks.† In another case, a man who, in his youth secured pleasure from reading of the 'whippings' in *Uncle Tom's Cabin*, liked to imagine himself domineered by a mistress, who, in his own words, "harnessed me to a carriage and made me take her for a drive, whom I must follow like a dog".‡

The mere fact of pleasurable submission to the other sex in the form of a sort of symbolic masochism may well develop into active masochism and end in definite perversion. Sexual passion for a member of the opposite sex, when intimately asociated with the wish to be dominated by, or tyrannised over, or 'henpecked' by the object of one's affections, is a dangerous

* Wilhelm Stekel, *Peculiarities of Behaviour*, Vol. I, p. 278.

† Krafft-Ebing, *Psychopathia Sexualis*, p. 186.

‡ *Ibid.*, p. 145.

state of mind to cultivate. It undoubtedly, in many cases, leads to masochistic practices.

There is always a possibility of whipping causing the development of masochism. The risks are largely governed by the age and sexual precocity of the youngster who is being punished. With the coming of puberty and during the years of adolescence, any form of corporal punishment bristles with dangerous potentialities and possibilities.

The self-revelatory confession of Rousseau is significant. When eight years old he was whipped by Mademoiselle Lambercier, and he experienced so much pleasure during the chastisement that, says Rousseau:

"It needed all the strength of this devotion and all my natural docility to keep myself from doing something which would have deservedly brought upon me a repetition of it; for I had found in the pain, even in the disgrace, a mixture of sensuality which had left me less afraid than desirous of experiencing it again from the same hand."*

This reaction on the part of the child was evidently discerned by Mlle Lambercier on the occasion of a subsequent whipping, for she "declared that it tired her too much, and that she would abandon it".

There would appear to be little doubt that the sexual perversion of the adult Swinburne, expressed in his anonymous *Whippingham Papers* and other publications, was fostered and developed by the floggings he received at Eton. Apropos of this, in his admirable study of Swinburne, Georges Lafourcade writes: "My impression is that Swinburne registered at Eton certain experiences, both in himself and in others, which were to have a great influence on his sexual development; but that it was only at a later date that he began to analyse, describe and magnify those early experiences which then became a sort of obsession."†

* *The Confessions of Jean-Jacques Rousseau*, 1896, p. 11.

† Georges Lafourcade, *Swinburne: A Literary Biography*, Bell, 1932, p. 48.

Every sexologist knows that the number of cases of individuals who have experienced sexual feelings while being whipped is a considerable one, and in nearly every instance where the anomaly has persisted in adult life the victim is able to trace the beginning of his perverse interest in flagellation to a flogging received at school or elsewhere.

Among the case-histories given by Havelock Ellis is that of a man who traced a connexion between "his first sexual thoughts and acts" and whipping.* Pfister gives the significant case of a girl of seven or eight who experienced feelings of pleasure when dreaming of being maltreated by a witch. She also liked to play, with children of both sexes, games in which scorching with a burning-glass and other punishments were involved, all of which gave her "great pleasure".†

It will serve no useful purpose to give further instances from the case-histories which besprinkle literature dealing with sexual pathology. Enough has been said to indicate the danger that the flogging of children may prove a means of exciting, stimulating or developing existent sexual precocity, or awakening erotic feeling where it is latent rather than positively active.

The possibility that corporal punishment in any form may induce sadism or masochism in those who are being flogged or the ones administering the punishment, cannot be overlooked or minimised. Years ago, when the wave of emotional indignation resulting from the white slave traffic exposures was causing a public demand for the increased use of the 'cat', Bernard Shaw drew attention to the connexion between sexual perversion and flogging, pointing out the sheer absurdity of imposing, as a punishment, a practice which the White Slave traffickers themselves adopted and exploited in the brothels. This connexion to which Shaw referred is a danger which always did exist and which always will.

So true is this, I cannot but feel that, in the past, those responsible for the ordering of penal floggings and other forms

* Havelock Ellis, *Studies in the Psychology of Sex*, Vol. III, Davis, Philadelphia, p. 289.

† Oskar Pfister, *The Psycho-analytic Method*, Kegan Paul, p. 162.

of corporal punishment, have unwittingly been the cause of the extension of sadism and masochism where these vices were present in their incipient stages, and for their creation and development in a considerable number of individuals who were previously quite untainted. In other cases, too, the callousness which seems, almost inevitably, to be a concomitant of association with or participation in any forms of corporal punishment, leads, sooner or later, to the fostering or extension of the cruelty that is so predominant a characteristic of human beings, and which finds its outlet in the torture of animals and birds.

No student of mankind who is actuated by humanitarian principles, and who has observed the effects and consequences of flagellation in its religious, educational, and penal forms, as set forth in the previous sections of this work, can but deplore the practice of a form of punishment so full of potentialities for all that is undesirable, evil and abominable.

Nor must one overlook the danger inseparable from the practice by the State of cruelty in any form. Man is by nature and training cruel enough in all conscience. He does not need the stimulating and fortifying influences of either precept or example. Every reformative measure of any true value has resulted from the efforts of a minority and not in response to the wishes of the masses. In many cases improvements have been effected which have been of no interest to the bulk of the people; in some cases, such improvements have been brought about in direct opposition to the wishes of the majority. To argue that because mankind is inherently cruel, corporal punishment as a punitive measure will never be abolished, is equivalent to contending that because the people of the civilised world are in favour of peace, war will never break out; that because man is naturally polygamous there can be no such thing as a practical system of monogamy. Cruelty, always dormant, is likely to become universal in times of stress and panic. It can only be kept in check by constant prophylactic and repressive measures. It is an essential feature of any State campaign against cruelty that torture shall form no weapon in its own armoury.

XIX: SUMMING-UP THE POSITION

APART from exceptional cases, penal flogging has disappeared from civilisation. Its primitiveness, its blatant and revolting cruelty, the risk it involves to life and limb, have sufficed to render it out of tune with the vaunted humanitarianism of the present age. There are, however, those who still hold that no form of punishment is so effectual as a corrective in the case of the criminal concerned, and as a deterrent in the case of others contemplating the commission of similar or analogous crimes; a view which would seem to be shared to some extent by the authorities themselves, *seeing that flogging has not yet been abandoned completely*.

In British judicial circles, for some decades, there was observable a reluctance to order, and in general circles, an antipathy towards, this form of punishment for any except the most brutal and horrible crimes. Especially was this antipathy observable in regard to the birching of children. At the same time, however, it was, and indeed still is, to a degree held by many that flogging is the only adequate punishment for certain forms of crime.

Such a conflict of opinion led in 1937 to the appointment, by the Home Secretary, of a Committee of Inquiry with a view to discovering in what directions reform of the law was necessary, and if any extension of the existing legal machinery for the infliction of corporal punishment was advisable.

In relation to the effects of corporal punishment the Committee said:

184

"It is essentially an unconstructive penalty. At the best, it can exercise no positive reformative influence; at the worst, it may produce reactions which make the individual who receives it less willing, or less able, than he was before to lead and honest and useful life in the community."

The Committee advocated the abolition of the birching of juveniles in any circumstances whatever; the abolition of the corporal punishment of adults under the Diplomatic Privileges Act, 1708;* the Knackers Act, 1786† the Vagrancy Acts of 1824 and 1873; for discharging or aiming a firearm at a sovereign; for importuning male persons; for procuration or living upon a woman's immoral earnings; and for garrotting and robbery with violence.

It was the opinion of the Committee that corporal punishment should be restricted to the punishment for certain prison offences; "mutiny, incitement to mutiny, and gross personal violence to an officer or servant of the prison". The Committee stated (page 114 of the Report):

"We are impressed by the unanimity with which the witnesses who have had practical experience of prison administration have stressed the necessity of retaining the power to impose corporal punishment for serious assaults on prison officers; and we have come to the conclusion that the time has not yet come when this power could safely be abandoned. We consider that it should be held in reserve as the ultimate sanction by which to enforce prison discipline; but we think that it should continue to be used very sparingly and we hope that in course of time, as the character of the prison population improves and there is less need for purely repressive measures,

* Section 4 of this Act provided for the infliction of corporal punishment upon any person instituting, or assisting in the prosecution of, certain actions at law against ambassadors or Ministers or their servants.

† Sections 8 and 9 of this Act provided for the public or private whipping of persons convicted of slaughtering horses and cattle without a licence or of destroying the hides of slaughtered animals.

it will be found possible to dispense altogether with the use of this form of punishment."

The recommendations of the Committee in regard to the abolition of flogging for all crimes, other than certain prison offences, were incorporated in a Bill placed before Parliament in 1939. Whether or not, in view of the flood of denunciation with which these humane proposals were greeted, the Bill would have succeeded in weathering the storm, there is no means of knowing, as the outbreak of war caused it to be placed on the shelf.

Towards the close of that year, however, the British public was shocked by the disclosures concerning the treatment of prisoners in Nazi concentration camps where, in circumstances reeking of brutality and callousness of the worst possible kind, the whip was in constant use. Twenty-five strokes inflicted on the buttocks with a rawhide whip was a common punishment, and sometimes as many as fifty were given.* These revelations induced a strong feeling against any form of punishment popular with those who ruled by terrorism and tyranny, and which, in its technique, was indistinguishable from torture.

In the years that followed, other factors contributed towards a change of viewpoint, even among many of those who had previously favoured flogging as a judicial measure, in regard to the desirability of retaining this form of punishment. This strong and mounting trend of public opinion against the birch and the 'cat' was shown in the protests voiced in Parliament against punishment by flogging in the Sudan, and against other extensions of the use of the whip. There had been several such extensions. Thus in 1942, in Jamaica, flogging was imposed as a punishment for the theft of growing crops; three years later, for a similar offence, corporal punishment, after its abolition in 1941, was reintroduced in Trinidad, while in Kenya, also in 1945, whipping, already a penalty for certain

* See *Papers Concerning the Treatment of German Nationals in Germany, 1938-1939*, H.M.S.O., London, 1939.

crimes, was extended to cover burglary and housebreaking. All these departures and experiments were subjected to severe criticism.

But it was the birching of young criminals in England itself that aroused the strongest protests. In 1943, much publicity was given to a case which 'spotlighted' one of the worst features of birching juvenile offenders. In accordance with the law in force at that time, when a Court of Summary Jurisdiction ordered a boy to be whipped, this punishment had to be given "as soon as practicable", and in the presence, should he wish to be present, of the boy's parent or guardian. Moreover, the parent or guardian had the right to appeal against the sentence. Now there could be no denying the justice of this right of appeal; but, at the same time, there could be no question that if the birching was to have the desired effect it must be inflicted immediately. Thus, because of their conflicting natures, one or the other of these equally important and desirable factors could not be carried out. If the culprit were to be whipped "as soon as practicable", in other words as expeditiously as possible, there could be no appeal. If the right of appeal were to be allowed, there must, of necessity, be an interval, which might conceivably be one of some weeks' duration, before the birching could be inflicted.

There can be little doubt that Press and public were beginning to frown upon the birching of juveniles. As time went on the sentences imposed by the courts became fewer. Viscount Templewood, in the course of a debate upon the Criminal Justice Bill in the House of Lords (June 29, 1948), put the position clearly:

"I believe I am right in saying that last year there were only twenty-five sentences of this kind [judicial whipping of young offenders under sixteen] in the inferior courts,* and that those sentences were given almost entirely by two or three Benches

---

* A Parliamentary question in 1943 had disclosed that in the previous year about three hundred birchings had been ordered by summary courts in England and Wales.

where these prejudices still exist. That seems to show that public opinion is against the continuance of this form of punishment."

In September, 1948, the Criminal Justice Act 1948 (11 & 12 Geo. 6, Ch. 58) came into operation. It abolished birching and flogging with the cat-o'-nine tails for all crimes other than certain prison offences, section 2 reading: "No person shall be sentenced by a court to whipping; and so far as any enactment confers power on a court to pass a sentence of whipping it shall cease to have effect." As regards prison offences, according to Part II, section 54, corporal punishment may be inflicted "for mutiny, incitement to mutiny, or gross personal violence to an officer of a prison when committed by a male person serving a sentence of imprisonment, corrective training or preventive detention". Such punishment "shall not exceed—

(a) in the case of a person appearing to the visiting committee or board of visitors or magistrate to be not less than twenty-one years of age, eighteen strokes of a cat-o'-nine-tails or birch rod; or

(b) in the case of a person appearing to them or him to be under that age, twelve strokes of a birch rod;

and if corporal punishment is inflicted, no further punishment by way of confinement in cells or restricted diet shall be imposed."*

Soon after the abolition of flogging, however, the increase in the incidence of crimes of violence, particularly of juvenile crime, and the use of the cosh, the bicycle chain and other fearsome weapons, once again caused a change of opinion in many quarters. Again and again did judges, in sentencing those guilty of crimes of violence, lament the fact that they could not order the criminals to be flogged. Again and again was it pointed out that coincident with the abolition of birching

* As mentioned earlier, corporal punishment for prison offences has now been abolished by the Criminal Justice Act, 1967.

there had, in some quarters, been a general increase in the degree of leniency displayed towards young offenders.

The call for the reintroduction of flogging was taken up by the Press, and there can be little doubt that persons in numbers and representative of all sections of society upheld this demand. A ballot taken by a popular newspaper revealed that those of its readers who recorded votes were overwhelmingly in favour of the reintroduction of both the birch and the 'cat'.

The members of the Magistrates' Association voted on the matter, giving a straight answer of "yes" or "no" to the question: "Are you in favour of courts having power to order corporal punishment for crimes of violence?" 9,294 papers were issued, 6,298 votes were given. The number in favour of the reinstatement of flogging was 4,412; the number against 1,886, giving a majority vote of 2,526 for corporal punishment. In February, 1953, however, the House of Commons, in a free vote, decided *against* the punishment of crimes of violence by flogging. The occasion was on the second reading of a Private Member's Bill to restore birching: the voting was 159 to 63.

There has probably never been an evil of any description for which it was not possible to dig up some argument in its favour, some excuse for its continued existence. The justification for the existence or extension of a practice lies not in the fact that it possesses certain virtues, but that those virtues outweigh its drawbacks, or that it serves society in some essential form for which there is no alternative method available.

By no species of argument can anything of this nature be claimed for corporal punishment. Its evils, its drawbacks, and its disadvantages, as we have seen in the process of our inquiry, outweigh hugely and in every possible way, its few supposed virtues—virtues which are based upon the most dubious foundations.

The true basis of any value which corporal punishment possesses as a preventive of crime is the fear which it instils in the culprit—actual or potential. Now fear is a powerful deterrent. It operates in the child, and in the adult, in the most primitive of races and in the highest strata of civilised society. But there are many kinds of fear. Fear of death is a necessary and valuable preventive of injury and suffering. Fear of displeasing one's parents is an admirable trait in the child. Fear of alienating public opinion, and fear of losing one's liberty or one's social position, are powerful antidotes to improper conduct and crime in adult society.

But the fear induced by corporal punishment belongs primarily to none of these categories. It is essentially and pre-eminently the fear of physical pain. It is the fear inevitably associated with suffering of a degrading, deliberate and debasing nature. Fear which is associated with and restricted to physical pain, as a punitive factor, possesses no *true reformative* power. Thus the qualities which commended corporal punishment to primitive and savage races, and which still appear to some as providing strong justification for its employment by the individual as a means of exacting private vengeance, become indefensible as applicable to any penological system of the modern State.

The individual, whether child or adult, who can be kept good or moral through fear of *personal suffering only*, is a pitiful creature. His reformation, or his good conduct, is purchased at a price which is as terrible as it is deplorable. His existence is that of a slave. In the time of the ancient Romans whipping was deemed to be a form of punishment more to be feared, because of its inherent degradation, than the death penalty. Its brand was emblematic of subjection of the basest kind. Through the centuries it lost few of its debasing features. Well might Lord Justice Mathew, the famous nineteenth-century dispenser of justice, say that "the lash is the punishment of the slave".

The dog which has been whipped into obedience is an object which can excite nothing but the most profound pity in every person who claims to possess any humane feelings at all. It is a cowed and dejected creature, and once it has been whipped into such a state the recovery of its former spirits and courage is impossible. It is exactly the same with the child or the man whose morality or reverence for law and order has been whipped into him. *If no other argument could be advanced against corporal punishment, then because of this one reason alone the case for its abolition would seem to be clear and complete.*

The argument which so often follows any proposal to abolish corporal punishment altogether that there is no other effectual method of punishing children to take its place is of dubious validity. There are, as Mr Walter Parsons, who had several years' experience as Chairman of Leeds Juvenile Court, pointed out, such effective methods as stopping the boy's pocket-money, or not allowing him to go to the cinema.* Nowadays, I suppose, he would be prevented from going to a football match or from watching his favourite programme on television.

It is just possible there may be a few exceptional cases where the flogging of an adult or the birching of a child is the best punitive treatment possible in the circumstances, but the difficulty lies in the selection of such cases. Few judges and fewer magistrates are in a position to exercise this selective power. Mr George F. Sleight, a specialist in the teaching of dull and backward children, and a pedagogue of much experience, once said that "the evil of corporal punishment was when a child was whacked without being made first to realise the justice of it".† Here precisely lies the difficulty. It is virtually impracticable, if not impossible, to make anyone, child or adult, recognise the justice of a flogging. On the contrary, flogging is almost certain to arouse in the individual who is punished, whatever be the nature of his offence, a feeling of being unjustly treated.

It has already been stated that in various quarters the fear was expressed that the abolition of the 'cat' and the birch would lead to an increase in the incidence of crime. Many factors have contributed, actually, towards the recent increase

---

* *Yorkshire Evening News*, August 4, 1937.

† *Manchester Guardian*, August 4, 1937.

in the incidence of violent crime, and especially of juvenile crime: the growing irresponsibility of and lack of control exercised by parents; the decline in religion, with a failure to make any clear-cut distinction between right and wrong; the marked decline in respect for the law; the glamourisation of toughness and gangsterism; and the powerful urge to continue, at any risk, the enjoyment of a once-tasted prosperity. Efforts to remove or to counteract these influences, even where they are successful, must necessarily be slow in producing results.

In the war upon crime, in any age and in any country, however, the main efforts of the State should be directed towards and concentrated upon proving to both the would-be as well as the practising criminal that illegal enterprises, in the huge majority of instances, are doomed to failure. The most severe punishment of the *unsuccessful* never deters the *successful* from repeating his crime, or the potential miscreant from becoming a criminal. Neither the one nor the other is thinking of failure, with punishment as an inevitable aftermath; on the contrary, he is confident of success. When the methods employed by the State are so efficient and so certain that anyone thinking of committing a criminal offence is well aware that detection and consequent punishment are almost inevitable, the conquest of crime will be well on the way to accomplishment. But not before.